Agency and Immigration Policy

Agency and Immigration Policy

Edited by

Simeon S. Magliveras

TRANSNATIONAL PRESS LONDON

2020

Migration Series: 28

Agency and Immigration Policy

Edited by Simeon S. Magliveras

Copyright © 2020 Transnational Press London

First Published in 2020 by TRANSNATIONAL PRESS LONDON in the United Kingdom, 12 Ridgeway Gardens, London, N6 5XR, UK.
www.tplondon.com

Transnational Press London® and the logo and its affiliated brands are registered trademarks.

Paperback
ISBN: 978-1-912997-67-1

Cover Design: Nihal Yazgan
Cover Image: Photo by Andrew Ridley at unsplash.com [andrew-ridley-jR4Zf-riEjI-unsplash]

www.tplondon.com

CONTENTS

ABOUT AUTHORS

Simeon S. Magliveras, PhD, is an Assistant Professor of Socio-cultural Anthropology in the Department of Global and Social Studies at the King Fahd University of Petroleum and Minerals, Saudi Arabia. He has done research and written about Greece and Albania, Southeast Asia, Laos and the Philippines, as well as, the Kingdom of Saudi Arabia. The general focus of his research has focused on movement of peoples resulting from political and economic upheavals and how ethnic and national identities are navigated and affected by the act of migration for both host and guests. His research also explores how transnational identities are maintained through collective memory, food and the senses.

Yahya Almasri is an Assistant Professor at the University of Hyogo, School of Economics and Management. His main research interests are in forced migration and Middle Eastern politics. He played a significant role in shaping the Japanese response to the higher education crisis in Syria in 2016 as one of the alternatives to refugee resettlement. Yahya is frequently invited to Japanese universities and high schools as a guest speaker.

Pavithra Jayawardena currently is a doctoral researcher at the Victoria University of Wellington, New Zealand. She is also a lecturer at the Department of International Relations, University of Colombo, Sri Lanka. Her research interests include migration, citizenship, Sri Lankan diaspora and diaspora relations with sending countries.

Georgia Lagoumitzi is Associate Lecturer in Sociology at the American College of Greece. She has taught a number of courses including collective behavior and social movements, the sociology of globalization, and supervises the senior thesis seminar. She has organized various conferences in Sociology and has been a member in the organizing committees of numerous others. She regularly contributes papers to conferences organized by the Hellenic Sociological Society (HSS). She presented papers on the Greek Diaspora in Oxford (2010), Athens (2013) and Bari (2019). She has presented papers in the American Studies Seminar, organized jointly by The American College of Greece and Panteion University (2011, 2019). Her publications include: "The Uses of Nostalgia in the 'Imagination' of the Diaspora: The Case of the New Pontic Greek Refugees" in Marianne David and Javier Muñoz-Basols (eds.), Defining and Re-defining Diaspora: From Theory to Reality (2011), "The Role of Public Sociology in the Pos-Truth Era", 6th HSS Conference Proceedings – e-book (2018)

Jera Lego is an independent researcher currently on semi-hiatus to raise a family. Her research interests include refugee politics, international organizations, and politics and international relations in Southeast Asia.

Previously she was a research associate at the Asian Development Bank Institute, a lecturer in the Comparative Politics of Southeast Asia, and a foreign affairs research specialist at the Center for International Relations and Strategic Studies at the Philippine Foreign Service Institute. She holds a PhD in Politics and International Relations from the International Christian University in Tokyo, Japan where she wrote her dissertation exploring themes of sovereignty, governmentality, and ambiguity in constructing the refugee category in the absence of national asylum frameworks in Southeast Asia.

Mathew Mathews, PhD, is Head of IPS Social Lab, a centre for social indicator research and a Senior Research Fellow in the Society and Culture Department at the Institute of Policy Studies, National University of Singapore. To date, Mathews has been involved in over forty research projects, most of them relating to issues in societal cohesion. These have included research using both quantitative and qualitative methods on areas such as race, religion, immigrant integration, family, ageing and poverty. Mathews also studies the impact of social programmes on social issues and has been involved in a number of evaluations on the usefulness of various government initiatives. He has taught courses on social policy and has published in a range of academic and media outlets.

Debbie Soon is research associate at Lee Kuan Yew School of Public Policy, Institute of Policy Studies, National University of Singapore.

CHAPTER 1

UNDERSTANDING POLICY IN IMMIGRATION

Simeon S. Magliveras

Introduction: Nature of Policy

Policies have become a form of social institution and are tools which governments use to organize contemporary societies (Shore and Wright 1995)[1]. The intensions and functions of organically formed institutions evolve as the social/biological environment changes through time but, policy in its genesis has specific intensions. Post-modernist thought avoid the nature of policy because it focuses of the individual and the individuals' ability to usurp power structures by avoiding categorization (Kirtsoglou 2004; Butler 2005). However, the nature and purpose of policy is to essentialize and categorize people and define subjects' access to power structures and determine individuals' roles and statuses in society (Shore and Wright 1995; Haines 2013). Thus, individuals are defined, enabled and limited by the categories policy imposes on them (as Citizen, refugee, legal/ illegal immigrant, etc). Thus, deeply embedded in policy are the cultural norms and ideologies, which help us understand power rhetorics and meanings of a society.

Policies, therefore, are not simply liturgical mechanism for government. Policies legitimize and channel activities and in turn objectify subjects. Subjects of policy thus become almost voiceless and invisible (Faucult 2012). It is also important to note that policy is a plan of action (Wedel et. al. 2005; Haines 2013) but for that plan to come to fruition it must fit into a context of moral constraints (Haines 2013). It can be argued that policy is not anymore separate from cultural norms, moralities, or politics than anything else. Policy should be plausible and appropriate to be effective (Haines 2013). But, social scientist have generally been critical of the motives behind policy. Rightly so, when actions taken are the detriment of particular groups. However, government policy often has unintended consequences.

On the one hand, policy is created to deal with the needs of society such as programs and laws created, for example, to alleviate poverty. On the other hand, often policy is created by government entities or influential organizations having particular agendas with particular concerned interests

---

[1] Policy contrast with other social institutions in that other institutions are a result of an organic process. Family for examples was not created out of intension but though an evolutionary process of trial and error. Policy is always created with intension

such as those governing pollution standards or the promotion of certain industries (Haines 2013). In other cases, policy is created to deal with social crisis such as the ever-present Covid19 pandemic. And in others cases, policy is a tool of social control or oppression. There is a plethora of reasons why a policy is created but one thing is certain, policy has become a major instrument of contemporary governance (Shore and Wright 1995)[2].

In this globalized world where neoliberal policies are making it easier for capital to move around the globe, in much of the literature migrating people are depicted as pawns in the neoliberal capitalistic game (Parrenas 2005; Paul 2017). However, rather than looking at immigrants as only passive groups on a metaphorical chess board, it is better to see them as both active and passive participants in the transnational world and immigration policy. These transnational individuals have cultures and morals which they bring with them and influence the people they meet. Transnationals irreversibly change the societies they visit and change the ones to which they return (Hann 2016). This book explores migration through the lens of this *policy nexus* (to be defined later in this introduction). It examines the relationship of hosts to guests and the relationship of emigrants to their places of origin. Immigration policy is made by powerful entities which force involved parties to make choices. According to Shore and Wright (1995), policy has a power of its own[3]. But what is the nature of policy and in particular what is the nature of immigration policy?

Policies are usually presented as standing above morality (Shore and Wright 1995). However, Shore and Wright (ibid.) infer that there is a tension and connection between morality and policy. This tension lies in the assumptions about morality where morality focuses on ethical issues and policy is framed as a mechanism for efficiency and pragmatism (Shore and wright 1995). Shore and Wright (1995) continue to suggest that this is but an illusion because below the surface of policy are idioms and metaphors which objectify decision making, restricting or denying human agency (Shore and Wright 1995). Thus, policy is based on particular moral imperatives and the people who must participate in the system are (de)valued, essentialized, envisaged, and 'created' through policy and moral interpretations. From a policy nexus perspective the morality of a society and the policy are intertwined agents affecting one another. Thus, policy should not be understood as simply an administrative process. So, as Shore and Wright and

---

[2] Okongwu and Mencher (2000) suggest the role of social scientist is to investigate the systems that create the situations and many inequities found today. They suggest that change is a result on a global scale where international and regional policy making institutions, states, multi-national quasi-governmental institutions, multinational private corporations shape economic and social policy (Madeley 1996; Bowles and Wagman 1997; Okongwu and Mencher 2000).

[3] Gell (1998) discusses how tools, objects which are made by human agents abducts the user in a particular way.

Foucualt suggest, the subjects of policy are silent (Shore and Wright 1995; Foucualt 2012) but are these actors not completely powerless? Power relations is also part of a policy nexus because the objects of policy are not passive powerless entities[4]. This introduction will define the immigration policy nexus then, examine the parts of the system. To better understand what is meant by the immigration policy nexus, Gells work on agency should be noted. Alfred Gell (1998) examined agency in the production and consumption of art.

Alfred Gell (1998) seminal work "Art and Agency" discusses the creation, production, interpretation, and consumption of art as a nexus of agents and agency. He analyses art from a perspective where the creator, the observer, and the object itself have agency. He does an ontological critical analysis of whom/what agency is. He defines an agent to be:

> "attributable to those persons (and things) who/which are seen as initiation causal sequences of a particular type, that is, events caused by acts of mind or will or intention, rather than mere concatenation of physical events. An agent[5] is one who 'causes things to happen ' in their vicinity" Gell 1998:16).

Gell envisages an agent not only as those who wheel power and appear at the obvious forefront to the creation of things but those who might seem to be passive observers who he considers to also be agents 'causing things to happen '. Interestingly, much of the vocabulary he uses to discuss art and agency is very similar to the language used by the literature describing policy and its characteristics. Gell discusses art in terms of agency, intension, causation, result, and transformation[6]. Likewise, discussants on policy describe policy similarly in that it is created with intension[7] and causation[8],

---

[4] Certainly, immigrants', as the object of policy, rights are restricted by policy and thus, would have limited agency than entities of power[4] but they are not denied it

[5] Gell (1998) goes on further to describe object or things as agents differently. Things can be agents if they initiate a causal sequence. Things as agents differs from human agents in that human agents create events through intension.

[6] Gell (1998) does an extensive semiotic analysis to construct his theories of agency. There are several terms he uses to frame his argument. A key term he discusses is the idea of the 'abduction of agency' which differs from an index (where smoke is an index of fire). "Abduction covers the grey area where semiotic inference (of meaning of signs) merges with 'hypothetical inferences' of a non-semiotic (or not conventionally semiotic) kind" p14. In other words, there is a grey area between indexical signs or natural signs, smoke meaning fire and index as an outcome of social agency where smoke is an index that someone started a fire, such as swidden agriculture. He suggests the smoke becomes an artefactual index, a tool and hence an index of agency.

[7] In Jayawardena chapter of this volume, she shows how the intensions of the government are different from the intensions of the return emigrants

[8] Almasari chapter in this volume discusses how a lack of political-cultural relations cause a liminal situation for Syrians refugees living in Japan refugee.

results and of course, transformation of individuals and society[9].

Policy is a confluence of many varied actors with different agendas. Legislators, lawyers, corporate interests, and constituents, just to name a few. Policy is then made into law and implemented by individuals in various government or social institutions and finally it is enacted upon people, specifically in the case of this volume, upon immigrants. Actors may have a very different intentions from the policy's creators but these actors are transformed by it[10]. Less obvious however, is that policy, becomes an agent of action by taking on a life of its own which may or may not result in the desired outcomes its creators[11]. The process of interacting agents is what this book terms the "policy nexus ". An immigration policy nexus therefore is an interaction of creators, enforcers, the actual policy and the people to which the policy is directed. With so many agents, policy becomes a fluid site and a site of political contestation (Wedel & Feldman 2005).

The contributions to this volume illustrate that policy is a complex nexus of agents: creators, the national and international influencers who are consulting, constructing, and writing policy, the subjects' interpretation and action with regards to policies and the policy as agent, as well as, either enforcers. Each agent has a different agenda and the nexus of these agents results in interesting and sometimes unpredictable consequences.

Immigration policy is interesting because seemingly powerless immigrants bare much of the brunt of said policies. Cultural idioms of us/them are unashamedly politicized at the expense of immigrants. Issues such as citizenship, human rights, labor rights, needs for laborer, culture and identity, all are intertwined into immigration policy. Policy, thus, becomes a tool of control and power. Moreover, immigrants and refugees are essentialized in everyday discourse as either hard working labors, or as lazy or immoral groups. They are politicized as barbarous caravans, or simply hordes of otherness. Immigrants are voiceless and at the same time burdened with all the ills of the host society. Much of the time, voices of their contributions are drowned out by the voices of fear and invasion. And this is inadvertently embedded in policy and its interpretations.

---

[9] Lagoumatzi in this volume illustrates how policy and the narratives of trauma transform the Greek narrative of national identity

[10] Shore and Wright (1995) suggest that policy categorizes individuals, determines there status and role increasingly "shaping and construction individuals" (p4).

[11] Gell (1998) defines two different types of agent, "agents" and "patients' Agents act and patients because of their existence are acted upon. Agents can be momentarily patients and vice versa. An example is a coffee table placed in front of an agent holding a cup. The agent places the cup on the table. The table is an agent making the cup holding person put the cup on the table but more specifically, the table is a patient because it is not doing the action. The patient, coffee table forces the agent to act giving the table's agency.

Book outline

This book is a selection of work from different places around the globe. It examines immigration and policy from different perspectives. Contributors to this this book explore the intention of policies, its causes, and the results of its enactment, to society's transformation but also it explores the action and agency of the subjects of said policies.

In chapter two of this book, Lego compares the refugee and asylum policies of Malaysia and Thailand. Using Foucault's perception about power and its inherent violent nature, Lego focuses on biopolitical rationality and understandings about the violence of sovereignty. She examines the different strategies both countries have for labour recruitment and labour migration but is critical of their violations of international customary law and lack of long term planning. The author also suggests there are signs of hope ending the chapter on a somewhat optimistic note.

In chapter three, Almasri examines the historical/political relationship of Japan and Syria and how that affects the refugee status of Syrians in Japan today. He explores the various agents which pressure the Japanese government to take note of refugees. However, because of ambiguous policies towards Syrian refugees, he found that Syrian who came to Japan with an informal refugee status live in Japan with limited rights. Moreover, since Syrian refugee policy is convoluted in Japan, Syrians and the civil servants dealing with their cases choose to give them an informal refugee status. Alsiri examines how this informal status has both positive and negative consequences.

Chapter four explores policies for returning emigrants from/to Sri Lanka from Australia and New Zealand. It examines the motivations and intentions of both government in creating policies for her returnees and the (mis)-understandings between the Sri Lankan government's understanding of returnees motivations and why returnees who choose to come back to Sri Lanka. Jayawardena explores the disconnect between the intensions of government returnee policy and the motivations of why emigrants return.

In chapter five, Mathew and Soon study naturalization policy in Singapore. They examine the selection process, procedures and justifications and model for naturalization of foreigners in Singapore. As much of life is Singapore, processes of naturalization is very unambiguous. The Singaporean government has created a system so that very specific ethnic, racial, and social statuses quotas are taken under consideration for those who want to become Singaporean. The chapter examines the 'Singaporean Citizen Journey, the discourses and symbols, and history used to create a feeling of identity in the 'ideal' new citizen

Chapter six explores how the national narrative and belonging are created in Greece. It explores collective traumas, historic amnesia, and the narratives of trauma, experienced by Pontiac Greeks in there expulsion from their home as a result of the 1923 Lausanne Treaty. Lagoumitzi shows how Greek government policy towards the Greek Pontiac diaspora transformed the refugees' incorporating them and their narratives of trauma into contemporary Greek society. The trauma of the Pontiac Greeks has become part of the national narrative to the contemporary Greek society.

Chapter seven of this book examines the nexus of various actors in the implementation of policy in Bahrain. The case study discusses how policies created for the benefit of guest workers in Bahrain. Guest workers must contend with powerful entities and social pressures, and cultural norms from home and from their host countries which gives subjects some options. These choices may appear illogical and self-defeating but they are choices made with particular objectives in mind. Magliveras focuses on the undertakings of a Filipino Overseas Worker and her agency; her choice to return to Bahrain even though her position was greatly compromised. It also examines her employer as an agent and the choices she made with regards to her Filipino worker. Finally it examines the policy as an agent and how it influenced these players; behaviors

Each submission examines international entities, governments, civil servants, employers, employees, refugees and policy, as agents. Each agent is part of a fluid process which crates, acts, and transform one another as part of the immigration policy nexus.

References

Butler, J. (2005), Giving an Account of Oneself, New York: Fordham University Press.

Gell, A. (1998). Art and Agency: an anthropological theory. Clarendon Press.

Foucault, M. (2012). Discipline and Punish: The birth of the prison. Vintage.

Haines, D. (2013). Migration, policy, and anthropology. International Migration, 51(2), 77-89.

Hann, C. M. (Ed.). (2016). When History Accelerates: essays on rapid social change, complexity and creativity. Bloomsbury Publishing.

Kirtsoglou, E. (2004). For the love of women: Gender, identity and same-sex relations in a Greek provincial town. Psychology Press.

Okongwu, A. F., & Mencher, J. P. (2000). The anthropology of public policy: shifting terrains. Annual Review of Anthropology, 29(1), 107-124.

Paul, A. M. (2017). *Agents of a New Transnationalization in the Migrant Domestic Worker Industry: Expanding the Transnational Migration Perspective*. Asia Research Institute, National University of Singapore.

Shore, Cris, and Susan Wright. (2003).Policy: A New Field of Anthropology (3-39), Shore, Cris, and Susan Wright, eds. Anthropology of policy: Perspectives on governance and power. Routledge.

Wedel, J. R., and Gregory Feldman. (2005). "Why an anthropology of public policy?" Anthropology Today 21.1: 1-2.

CHAPTER 2

CRIMINALIZED AND VULNERABLE: REFUGEES AND ASYLUM SEEKERS IN THAILAND AND MALAYSIA

Jera Lego

Malaysia and Thailand together host the largest number of refugees and asylum seekers in Southeast Asia, despite not having acceded to the 1951 Convention Relating to the Status of Refugees, nor its 1967 Protocol, and without having a national asylum framework. In the absence of any legal protection relating to their status, those refugees and asylum seekers are subject to harsh immigration laws as any undocumented migrant. Moreover, they are drawn into the same labor conditions and immigration crackdowns without the benefit of protection from any state to which they might claim to be a citizen of. This chapter examines those labor and immigration policies and their implications for the plight of refugees and asylum seekers in Thailand and Malaysia. It begins with Malaysia's efforts to manage labor migration, followed by a discussion of related immigration policies and their implications for the protection and welfare of undocumented migrants, and especially of refugees and asylum seekers. The situation in Thailand will then be considered in the same manner. The chapter concludes with a comparison of the policies and situation of refugees and asylum seekers in the two countries.

Malaysia

As a result of close links and porous borders with neighboring countries and segmented labor markets, several hundred Indonesians were already working in rubber and oil plantations in Johor while Thais were seasonally employed in sugar plantations in Perlis and padi fields in Kedah in the 1970s, long before there were any domestic labor shortages (Pillai, 1999). Malaysia's New Economic Policy (NEP) begun in the 1970s and its focus on urbanization and industrialization eventually caused labor shortages in the rural areas, particularly in the agricultural sector, and later on in the construction and services sectors, attracting a growing number of foreign workers. By the 1980s, Malaysia was said to have become a country of immigration but without any clear policy program. These earlier migration flows, were largely unregulated, undocumented, or to use Batistella's term, 'unauthorized' (Batistella, 2004: 203).

Malaysia's recent Labour Force Surveys estimate that foreign migrant workers account for about 15% of a 15 million-strong labor force (Loganathan, et.al., 2019; World Bank, 2019), roughly 2.25 million foreign migrant workers in total. Precise figures are harder to come by. A study by the ISEAS-Yusof Ishak Institute estimates the population of foreign migrant workers in Malaysia at anywhere between 3.85 to 5.5 million as of 2016 (Lee & Khor, 2018) while a study by the World Bank puts the number between 2.96 million to 3.26 million in 2017, of which irregular foreign workers number 1.23 million to 1.46 million. As of 2017, the top sources of migrant labor in Malaysia were Indonesia, Nepal, Bangladesh, India, and Myanmar (ILO, 2018).

Efforts to Manage Labor Migration

Kassim and Zin narrate how this unregulated entry of foreign worker came to be viewed as a growing threat to internal political stability especially as the number of foreign migrants grew more visible in construction and services sectors in urban areas (Kassim & Zin, 2011). In response to this perceived threat, the Malaysian government began to centralize policies and regularize the recruitment of migrant workers. In 1982, a Committee for the Recruitment of Foreign Workers was established to formulate migration policies, later renamed the Cabinet Committee for Foreign Workers in 1991 (Devadason & Chan, 2011). In 1984, a landmark labor pact, known as the Medan Agreement, was signed with Indonesia, historically Malaysia's largest source of labor. The agreement requiried prospective employers to go through official channels, i.e., through Malaysia's Ministry of Home Affairs, Ministry of Labour, Immigration Department, and Indonesia's Ministry of Manpower (Kassim, 1987). Over time, various agreements were signed with different countries such as the Philippines, Bangladesh, Thailand, China, Vietnam, and Pakistan allowing recruitment from those countries for different sectors through private employment agencies (Devadason & Chan, 2011:5-6). Kassim writes that these early attempts to control the flow of migrant labor were ineffective, particularly of those from Indonesia. In interviews with the Ministry of Home affairs, she was told, "prospective employers, and especially prospective migrants, deplore bureaucratic procedures which are time-consuming and incomprehensible to the Indonesian layman" (Kassim, 1987: 268).

The government also attempted to use market-based measures to curb recruitment of migrant workers, particularly unskilled ones. In 1991, an annual levy was imposed on all migrant workers depending on which industry they were in and whether they were engaged in skilled, semi-skilled, or unskilled work. These levies came to be a significant source of revenue, earning for the state about 430 million ringgit[1] in 1996 (Pilllai, 1999: 183). Another market-based measure introduced was mandatory contributions by employers to an Employees' Provident Fund (EPF) in 1998. While aimed at discouraging the recruitment of migrant workers, these policies only backfired as employers resorted to hiring foreign workers illegally and underreporting wages in order to decrease contributions to the EPF (Devadason & Chan, 2011). The EPF was eventually revoked in 2001 but the levies were subsequently increased at various times for different sectors such as in 1995, 1998, and 2005. In 2009, the government decided that the levy was to be paid for by employers rather than the migrant workers but the burden was again shifted back to migrant workers in 2013 (The Malaysian Insider, 2013). The levy, along with visa and processing fees, were too costly for poorly paid migrant workers, that it prevented migrant workers from registering with the authorities and legalizing their status. Moreover, work permits had to be renewed annually; many failed to do so because of the cost and wind up reverting to their illegal status after a year (Kassim & Zin, 2011: 25).

Meanwhile, hiring bans were imposed time and again during economic downturns only to be lifted once employers complain of labor shortages. For instance, a freeze on 'labor importation' (employers could still hire from immigration detention depots) was imposed in the wake of the 1997 Asian Financial Crisis and was later lifted in 1998, allowing for the issuance of 120,000 new work permits in the plantation and construction sectors. In 2009, in the wake of the Lehman shock and global financial crisis that ensued, a hiring freeze in manufacturing was imposed, only to be lifted after six months following complaints by employers of cancelled international orders due to labor shortages. In some cases, the government even allowed the immediate re-migration of deported workers to alleviate labor shortfalls (Devadason & Chan, 2011).

The Malaysian state has thus since the 1980s attempted to centralize labor migration policies, formalize the status of foreign migrant workers, and at the same time discourage hiring of those foreign migrant workers, all with little success. Both employers and prospective migrant workers continued to utilize illegal and informal agents. Kassim's interviews are quite telling: employers and migrant workers alike 'deplored' bureaucratic procedures and found it 'incomprehensible' such that, at the time of writing that article, only 200 Indonesians had been recruited under the terms of the Medan Agreement (Kassim, 1987: 268). Attempts to discourage the recruitment of foreign workers using mandatory contributions and levies have been

---

[1] Worth roughly, US$172 million in 1996 at 1MYR=0.4USD from http://fxtop.com/en/historical-exchange-rates.php accessed 3 January 2016.

ineffective. Rather, they undermined efforts to regularize the status of migrant workers but with the added benefit of providing a huge source of revenue for the state. Meanwhile, there does not seem to be any coherent connection with a comprehensive labor policy. Hiring bans are lifted not long after they are implemented suggesting a highly reactive rather than a proactive program of labor governance. There appears to be a need to reconcile policies for addressing unemployment among the local population, employers' preference for cheap foreign labor, and perceived security concerns. Indeed, much of the literature on migration research in Malaysia is critical of the state's policy incoherence towards labor migration, the country's dependence on foreign workforce, and the social and economic consequences of mismanagement (Wong, 2002). Devadason has even described the combination of weak regulatory framework, the lack of cooperation between stakeholders, and conflicting views on labor market needs that characterize the management of migrant workers as 'chaos in the house' (Devadason & Chan, 2011: 4-8). It is also worth noting Pillai's hypotheses why such a state of 'chaos' exists: corruption in the 'immigration industry' involving Malaysian immigration officials, 'turf wars' among the various bureaucracies, further complicated by politicians' compulsion to respond and do something about perceived dangers such as the threat that foreign migrant workers bring with them (Pillai, 1999: 183-184).

In the midst of Malaysia's labor market characterized by both a huge demand for low-wage labor and incoherent policies that simultaneously try to satisfy and discourage such demand, documented and undocumented migrant workers alike face significant barriers to affordable healthcare. A recent study by Loganathan, et. al. (2019) found that migrant workers are deterred by costly fees, fear of arrest and deportation, as well as language barriers and discrimination when attempting to access healthcare. Public healthcare is highly subsidized for citizens but are much more expensive for non-citizens.[2] As a result, undocumented migrants may falsify documents. Moreover, patients at public health facilities are routinely asked to produce legal documents such as passports and work permits at registration counters of public health facilities. Malaysia's Ministry of Health (MOH) directs all health professionals to report the presence of undocumented foreigners to the police, as required by the Immigration Act and some public hospitals have police and immigration counters located on their premises. Lastly, migrant workers, even with proper documentation, experience harassment and extortion by the police en route to public health facilities, even those going by taxi. All these serve to prevent migrant workers from receiving

---

[2] Price difference was over forty times for outpatient treatment and over a hundred times for in-patient treatment (Loganathan, et.al., 2019).

timely medical attention or avoid hospital care altogether.

Criminalizing Undocumented Migrants

As Malaysia attempts to manage labor migration, a parallel program to criminalize irregular or undocumented migration is also being implemented. Malaysia's Immigration Act of 1959/63 allows significant powers to immigration and police officers in arresting and detaining suspected illegal immigrants. Section 51(1) provides that any immigration or police officer may "without a warrant" […] "enter and search any premises; or stop and search any vessel, vehicle or person" […] "if he has reason to believe that any evidence of the commission of an offence against this [Immigration] Act is likely to be found." Section 51(5) b also provides that non-citizens may be held for up to 14 days before being presented to a Magistrate who "shall make an order for his detention for such period as may be required by an immigration officer or a police officer for the purpose of investigations into an offence against this Act, or by an immigration officer for the purpose of either making inquiries, or effecting his removal from Malaysia, under this Act." Section 34 (1) states that any person who is ordered to be removed from Malaysia under the Immigration Act "may be detained in custody for such period as may be necessary for the purpose of making arrangements for his removal." In other words, undocumented migrants in Malaysia are vulnerable to arbitrary arrest and indefinite detention.

While strict rules were already in place allowing for broad policing power of suspected illegal migrants, the Malaysian public, as mentioned earlier, increasingly saw foreign migrant workers as a threat as they became more visible in the in the 1980s. In response to this growing concern, the Home Affairs Minister announced in 1985 a nationwide campaign to crackdown on 'illegal' migration. The Malaysian task force on refugees known as Task Force VII was given extra powers to deal with illegal immigrants by identifying landing points and increasing patrolling activities at those points. The police, navy, air force, and the People's Volunteer Corps (Ikatan Relawan Rakyat, also known as *RELA*) were directed to cooperate with Task Force VII and the general public was also enjoined to cooperate (Kassim, 1987: 269). This early involvement of a task force originally intended to deal with refugees suggests Malaysia's migration and refugee policy are in fact deeply intertwined.

In the 1990s, at the same time that regulations regarding foreign migrant workers were being put in place, the Malaysian government also began strengthening border control and surveillance. *Ops Nyah* 1[3] which consisted of land and maritime border control and surveillance exercises, began on 1

---

[3] *Ops Nyah* can be loosely translated as Operation 'Expunge' or Operation 'Get Rid.'

January 1992 and followed by *Ops Nyah 2* implemented in July of the same year. This involved arresting illegal immigrants, detaining them at immigration detention centers, and thereafter sentenced to a fine, jail, and/ or caning, and once the sentence is served, deported. Numerous other immigration crackdowns and deportation exercises have been implemented since then (Devadason & Chan, 2011; Kassim & Zin, 2011). A total of 1.2 million undocumented foreigners were identified under Ops Nyah 1 and Ops Nyah 2 between 1993 and 1997 (HDSPLU, 2013: 122). Under criticism from rights groups and also noting the ineffectivity of crackdowns and deportation exercises, the Malaysian government began implementing amnesty exercises (*Program Pengampunan*) prior to crackdowns starting in 1996. Illegal or irregular immigrants were given a period of time to leave the country without being charged for violating immigration laws. Various exercises have been implemented since then including in 1997, 1998, 2002, and in 2004-2005 (Kassim & Zin, 2011).

In the wake of the Asian Financial Crisis in 1997, public sentiment towards foreign migrant workers only worsened. The Immigration Act was amended in 1997 to increase the fine for hiring foreign workers without permits from 5,000 ringgit to a maximum of 10,000 ringgit and imprisonment from one to five years upon conviction. Even then the effectiveness of fines, raids, and deportation exercises in curbing illegal migration appeared dubious. At least one study has found that irregular migrants who return to their home country voluntarily are able to return to Malaysia under a different name while those who are regularized soon become illegal after failing to renew their (costly) permits (Kassim et al., 2014: 253).

In 2002, a riot by foreign workers at a textile plant led the Enforcement Division of the Department of Immigration to identify irregular migrants as 'Public Enemy No.2,' next only to drug addiction (Kassim et al., 2014: 252). That same year, the Immigration Act of 1959/63 was further amended to enforce tougher rules on illegal immigrants. Section 6 (3) provides that anyone found guilty of illegal entry into Malaysia is shall be "be liable to a fine not exceeding ten thousand ringgit or to imprisonment for a term not exceeding five years or to both, and shall also be liable to whipping of not more than six strokes." In 2003 alone, following these amendments to the Immigration Law, some 42,900 undocumented migrants were arrested, 9,000 of whom received corporal punishment (Kaur, 2008: 14). Within two years of the 2002 amendment, an estimated 18,000 undocumented migrants were whipped (Nah, 2007: 40).

As mentioned earlier, paramilitary volunteer corps known as RELA is also involved in arresting, detaining, and deporting migrants. RELA was established in 1972 under the force of the Section 2 of Emergency (Essential Powers) Act of 1964. In 2005, the Act was amended to expand RELA's powers to include arrest and detention of undocumented migrants, as well as the right to bear and use firearms, stop, search and demand documents, arrest without a warrant, and enter premises without a warrant, when the RELA personnel has reasonable belief that any person is a terrorist, undesirable person, illegal immigrant or an occupier (FIDH-SUARAM, 2008:11). It is worth mentioning that Malaysian civil society and human rights groups have long expressed serious concern for such wide discretionary powers being given to untrained civilian corps and their role in perpetrating human rights abuses against undocumented migrants (AI, 2010; ERT, 2010; FIDH-SUARAM, 2008; Hedman, 2008; Garces-Mascarenas, 2015). These concerns finally came to a head when, in March 2012, a Nigerian student was allegedly beaten to death by RELA members (AI, 2013: 16). A month later, the Malaysian Parliament passed the Malaysia Volunteer Corps Bill 2012 that stripped RELA of the right to bear firearms and to conduct their own raids. Still, some members of civil society are not satisfied. Ismail writes that the Act may have disallowed RELA from carrying firearms but it also enhances RELA's capacity building, leadership structure, and training thus making it better established (Ismail, 2012). To date, RELA has about three million members, a team in each of Malaysia's 156 districts, including taxi drivers who are "to eavesdrop on their passengers' conversations and report to the police if they hear anything suspicious" (Nadaraj, 2013). Indeed, even without the RELA carrying firearms, Malaysia's legal framework provides the state's various officials wide, discretionary powers in policing, arresting, detaining and deporting irregular or undocumented migrants. Hedman and Nah have both described Malaysia's immigration crackdowns as public performances of sovereignty that are meant to reify the state and articulate a distinct Malay identity (Hedman, 2008; Nah, 2012). While on the one hand, the state tries, often unsuccessfully, to manage, regularize and gather information on undocumented migrant workers by allowing them to register and granting them amnesty, highly punitive measures are in place which encourage foreign migrants to evade state authorities, subjecting them to abuses in the hands of private actors all the same.

Impact on refugees and asylum seekers

Since the 1970s, Malaysia has witnessed two major refugee influxes. First was the outflow of Cambodian, Lao, and Vietnamese refugees fleeing in the aftermath of US withdrawal from South Vietnam and its surrender to North Vietnam. Under the so-called Comprehensive Plan of Action (CPA) facilitated by the UNHCR, Malaysia hosted more than 250,000 of those Indochinese refugees and asylum seekers, of which more than 240,000 were later resettled in third countries (Robinson, 1998). A second group of refugees and asylum seekers, many of them fleeing conflict, violence, and persecution in Myanmar, began arriving in peninsular Malaysia in the 1980s and have since steadily increased in number. As of November 2019, there were some 178,100 refugees and asylum seekers registered with the UNHCR in Malaysia, of which around 153,430 are from Myanmar, and the rest from Pakistan, Yemen, Somalia, Syria, and Afghanistan, among others (UNHCR Malaysia, 2020).

As mentioned earlier, Malaysia does not have national asylum framework that could provide a legal basis for recognizing refugees and any rights that accrue to such a status. As a result, refugees and asylum seekers are viewed as illegal immigrants subject to arrest, detention, imprisonment, corporal punishment, and deportation. On occasion, Malaysia has exempted certain groups from such penalties on the basis of Section 55 (1) of Malaysia's Immigration Act 1959/63 which provides that "the Minister may by order exempt any person or class of persons, either absolutely or conditionally, from all or any of the provisions of this Act". This has been the legal basis for issuing a temporary residence permit called the IMM13 card or permit. IMM13 holders are allowed to remain legally in Malaysia, engage in lawful employment, register their children in government schools and to access public services. The permit must be renewed annually for a certain fee and can be cancelled at the Minister's discretion. While the decision to grant IMM13 permits is to be based on information provided by the applicant concerning their reasons to seek for exemption, in practice, the precise criteria is unknown and there is no way for the applicant to challenge the decision of the Minister (FIDH-SUARAM, 2008).

Malaysia has granted IMM13 permits to certain groups such as the Acehnese Muslims fleeing conflict between the Indonesian military and the Free Aceh Movement in 2005. However, in order to receive recognition as a refugee, asylum seekers must register with the UNHCR and undergo a refugee status determination (RSD) procedure. Elsewhere I have documented this lengthy and tedious procedure, the various difficulties that asylum seekers encounter in the process, as well as the difficulties faced by the UNHCR in adjudicating those claims while attempting to provide some protection and assistance with the help of local nongovernment organizations (NGOs) and refugee community organizations (RCOs) (Lego, 2012). Asylum seekers could be waiting up to two years for the result of their RSD application and an even longer time to be resettled in a third country were they to succeed in their application. Within that time, in the absence of an IMM13 permit, refugees and asylum seekers have no work permit, no source of income, and are therefore forced to work illegally, leaving them vulnerable to exploitation by unscrupulous employers, with poor access to healthcare and education for their children, and subject to penalties related to their status as illegal immigrants.

Fortunately for refugees and asylum seekers, the UNHCR, NGOs, and

RCOs advocate for their protection and provide some material assistance. Human rights organizations such as Amnesty International, the Asia Pacific Refugee Rights Network, Equal Rights Trust, SUARAM, and Tenaganita openly call on the Malaysian government to recognize the rights of refugees (as well as the rights of migrants), sometimes even intervening specific cases of arrest and detention of refugees and asylum seekers. Other NGOs and RCOs provide temporary shelter, healthcare services, education for children, training for adults, and other forms of assistance primarily to refugees and asylum seekers who possess documents from either the UNHCR or their respective RCO. Unfortunately, not all refugee groups have RCOs through which they may avail of some assistance and protection. Other NGOs also have limited resources and do not always have the cooperation of the police or immigration authorities. The UNHCR is sometimes able to secure the release of refugees and asylum seekers from detention but this could take months or even years (APRRN, 2018a). Generally, refugees and asylum seekers, especially those who have not yet registered with the UNHCR are subject to arrest, detention, imprisonment, and deportation. The latter is particularly problematic because refugees and asylum seekers, by definition, are unable to avail of the protection of their country of their origin— deporting them is therefore highly likely to amount to refoulement or returning them to a place where they might suffer persecution or violence. Refugees and asylum seekers arriving in Malaysia are thus faced with hostile immigration policies which (1) criminalize illegal entry and their mere presence on Malaysian soil as with any undocumented migrant worker, (2) penalize them for making a living, (3) offer little or no material welfare or assistance (e.g., health and education) except by intervention of the UNHCR and NGOs, and (4) place them at risk of being returned to the same dangers they were fleeing from in the first place. In May 2018, a new coalition government came to power in Malaysia, ending the 60-year rule of Barisan Nastional. The new government has committed to ratifying the 1951 Convention Relating to the Status of Refugees in their manifesto and in November 2018 announced that the Cabinet would decide on allowing refugees the right to work. At the time of writing, it remains to be seen whether such promises will come to fruition.

THAILAND

Like Malaysia, Thailand has experienced rapid economic growth that has created a huge demand for low-cost labor, increased wages, and drawn migrant workers from neighboring countries. The UN Thematic Working Group on Migration in Thailand puts the number of non-Thai population living and working in Thailand at about 4.9 million as of November 2018. Of these, over 3 million are low-skilled workers from Cambodia, Laos, Myanmar, and Vietnam with work permits; some 800,000 are low-skilled workers from Cambodia, Laos, Myanmar, and Vietnam with irregular status; and over 100,000 are refugees, asylum seekers, and people living in refugee-like situations. This puts the share of migrant workers at over ten percent of Thailand's total labor force (Smith, Lim, and Harkins, 2019). Like Malaysia, Thailand struggles to develop coherent labor migration policies, regularize the status of different categories of migrant workers, and formalize recruitment channels. Thailand's migration policies are also characterized by an emphasis that migration should be on a temporary basis.

Managing Labor Migration

Thailand in the 1980s saw massive rural to urban migration that created a huge demand for cheap labor in agricultural and other labor-intensive sectors in the rural areas. By the late 1980s, Thailand had transitioned from being a net exporter to a net importer of migrant workers. In 1988, based on Article 17 of the Immigration Act 1979, the Thai Government relaxed its strict immigration policy and allowed undocumented migrants from Cambodia, Laos, and Myanmar to work 'legally' on a temporary basis (Archavanitkul & Hall, 2011). By the 1990s, smuggling networks flourished facilitated by the porosity of borders and indirect support from some corrupt government officials (Hall, 2011). In 1996, the Thai government then began implementing 'quasi-regularization' of migration out of concern to meet labor demand while safeguarding national security. 'Quasi-regulation' involved registering migrant workers (Chalamwong, Meepien, & Hongprayoon, 2012) as well as moves to relax prohibitions on migrant workers (Chantavanich, 2007).

Beginning in 1996, Cabinet resolutions were being issued every year mandating legal registration of migrant workers (Archavanitkul & Hall, 2011). Quasi-regularization of migration by means of Cabinet resolutions meant that 'illegal' workers could register legally to work for one to two years as 'labourers' or as 'domestic servants'. Once registered, a worker's status remained, somewhat confusingly, 'illegal, pending deportation' due to illegal entry (Hall, 2011). In other words, the label 'illegal' remained due to the migrant's mode of entry into Thailand regardless of having received valid documentation that exempts the migrant from arrest and immediate deportation.

Between 2002 and 2003 (renewed in 2015-2016), under the initiative of the National Security Council (NSC), Thailand signed Memoranda of Understanding (MOU) to formalize recruitment channels for migrant workers coming from Cambodia (May 2003), Laos (October 2002), and Myanmar (June 2003). By the end of 2010, less than 80,000 migrant workers had entered the country through these formal processes established under the MoUs (Huguet & Chamratrithirong, 2011: xii). In 2003, the NSC also designated the Ministry of Labor (MOL) to lead in developing policies for legalizing or regularizing irregular migrants (Chalamwong, Meepien, & Hongprayoon, 2012; Hall, 2011). Chalamwong and others describe this period between 2001-2003 as characterized by a 'half-open door policy' whereby the Thai government extended the registration policy but only for some sectors and some provinces (Chalamwong, Meepien, & Hongprayoon, 2012).

In 2004, the Thai government began issuing so-called Tor Ror 38/1 documents with 13-digit numbers that served as certification for registration of temporary stay and the possibility for obtaining a work permit to be renewed annually and subject to passing a medical examination. Since then, registered migrants were to have three documents: Tor Ror 38/1, a health insurance card, and a work permit (Thaweesit & Napaumporn, 2011). Two other procedures were initiated in the same year—the so-called Nationality Verification (NV) procedure and the 'import' of workers with temporary passports directly from neighboring countries (Chalamwong, Meepien, & Hongprayoon, 2012; Hall, 2011). NV was implemented beginning in 2009 for migrant workers from Myanmar and 2006 for migrant workers from the Cambodia and Laos who had originally entered Thailand 'illegally' to verify their nationality in their home countries as prerequisite to obtaining a work permit in Thailand. Migrants needed to provide personal data to home countries for verification to receive a temporary passport or a certificate of identity, a visa to remain in Thailand, and legal work status (Hall, 2011). Migrants who pass the NV procedure were to be exempted from arrest or deportation and allowed to travel to any province in Thailand as well as back to their home countries. They can only extend their permit for up to four years, however, wait three years before they can reapply for employment in Thailand, and report to an immigration office every 90 days (Archavanitkul & Hall, 2011). By the end of February 2011, about only 550,000 migrant workers had completed this process (Huguet & Chamratrithirong, 2011: xii). Thai PBS reported on 23 March 2015 that of the 1.6 million migrant workers from Cambodia, Laos, and Myanmar, about only 200,000 have had their nationalities verified. Delays in nationality verification, according to the director-general of the Employment Department, stemmed from two factors: inadequate officials from the three countries who were sent to Thailand to help in the verification process and the workers themselves do not have proper documents (Thai PBS, 23 March 2015). Research by the Migration Policy Institute also reveals financial barriers to using formal migration channels. Whereas the typical Cambodian would need to pay $700 for documents and fees, and wait three to six months for approval, traveling with a broker would cost only $100 to $150 and can be arranged within days (Bylander & Reid, 2017).

The effort to manage Thailand's irregular migrant population is therefore a relatively recent program for which coherent objectives and a long-term approach were yet to be defined. It is somewhat surprising that registration exercises only began in 1992 when Thailand had already become a net importer of migrant workers since the late 1980s. It suggests reactiveness rather than deliberate policymaking. It is also revealing that for more than a decade after that, permission to stay for hundreds of thousands of migrant workers was granted by Cabinet decision on a yearly basis. This seems to imply an expectation that the demand for migrant labor would later be addressed by some other means, that the migrant population would then return, or perhaps even a denial of the importance of migrant labor population for the Thai economy. This perception that migrant workers were just a temporary feature of Thai economy, detached as it is from reality, is also evident in the persistent use of the term 'illegal.' As mentioned earlier, categories exist of legal and illegal migrant workers who both possess documents and are granted permission to work—the difference being that illegal migrant workers are those who entered Thai territory through informal channels. It appears as though those who formulate these policies have little understanding of the porosity of Thailand's borders and/ or its capacity to police these borders. The fact that those 'registered illegal' migrant workers are allowed to work pending their deportation only testifies to the great demand for such migrant labor. At the same time, it reveals that the category for legality in Thailand is not so much a function of recognition by the government than one of deportability. Migrant workers are considered illegal despite documentation and permission to stay. Rather, they are illegal as the state reserves the right to remove them from Thai soil after a certain period. Two other factors appear to have become part of the criteria for defining illegality and deportability: successfully completing a medical examination and verifying one's nationality. Here, a biopolitical rationality for managing populations is evident. Anything less than a healthy body that is useful for the Thai economy can be deported. Meanwhile, an identifiable nationality is also prerequisite, regardless of the fact that the Thai economy has already benefited from the labor of migrant workers. Great discrepancies between the turn out for initial and subsequent registration procedures testify to shortcomings in effectively managing the migrant labor economy. It is also telling that the Thai government would require migrants form Myanmar to return and/ or obtain some sort of verification from the military junta which many of them are likely fleeing from for reasons other than to seek better livelihood.

Derks' interview with a Cambodian migrant workers conducted in Thailand in 2007 is illustrative of the utter ineffectiveness of efforts to regularize labor migration in Thailand:

He [a Cambodian migrant worker] had had a registration card during his first year of work in Chonburi, but his boss missed the deadline for its extension. He has since worked without documentation. His current employer in Rayong told me [Derks] that he did not even consider registering his migrant workers, because he was never sure about the next construction project. Although he [the employer] was very pleased with the work and meekness of his Cambodian workers, this employer knew that, as soon as he had no more work to offer them, they would move on to another employer. He would lose any money invested in their registration. Therefore, instead of registering his migrant workers, Phirun's employer paid a monthly sum to individuals from the immigration department, to the police and to a high-ranking local official. In return, he was warned in advance of police raids, in time for him to hide his undocumented workers (Derks, 2013:224).

The interview above reveals how cumbersome regulations have been for both migrant workers and employers, how both migrant workers and employers opt to utilize other strategies for evading those regulations and law enforcement authorities, and how state authorities themselves are undermining efforts to manage and enforce migration policies.

Criminalizing irregular migrant workers

Meanwhile, the past decade or so has seen a move to criminalize irregular migrant labor. In 2008, a new Alien Working Act B.E. 2551 came into force which provided that an alien working without a work permit is subject to imprisonment for a period of up to five years and/or a fine of 2,000 baht to 100,000 baht. Employees with work permits must contribute to the so-called Alien Out-of-Kingdom Repatriation Fund to be used, among other things, to pay for the cost of deportation of 'aliens' who do not use their own funds to leave Thailand (Thailand Law Forum, 2009). The Act also introduced levies for employing migrant workers in specific sectors and areas, reduced fees in border areas to encourage migrants to stay there, offered rewards to those who notify authorities about undocumented workers, and permitted law enforcement officials to enter establishments suspected of hiring undocumented workers and arrest those undocumented workers even without warrants (Hall, 2011).

In May 2014, a military government came to power whose approach to migration was even more restrictive. One of its first official announcements was to arrest and deport any irregular migrant worker found in Thailand. This triggered the departure of more than 250,000 Cambodians fearful of a harsh crackdown over the course of just three weeks. This sudden loss of a significant migrant workforce led to labor shortages, construction delays, and production cuts, exposing Thailand's structural dependence on low-wage migrant labor (Bylander & Reid, 2017). In response, the Thai government opened a new window for registering irregular migrant workers, for which some 1.6 million migrant workers in fact turned out and registered (Harkins, 2019).

In June 2017, as part of a comprehensive new law on labor migration, the Thai government announced the Royal Ordinance on the Management of Foreign Workers Employment B.E. 2560 (2017). It was hoped the law would bring clarity and coherence in Thailand's labor migration framework. Instead, it emphasized harsh measures intended to encourage use of formal channels (Harkins, 2019). Among others, it (1) re-imposed fines of 2,000 to 100,000 baht (US$60 to US$3,000) and/ or imprisonment of up to five years for workers without proper documentation, (2) imposed fines of 400,000 to 800,000 baht (US$12,000 to US24,000) per unauthorized worker for employers, and (3) introduced penalties of up to 100,000 baht and/ or imprisonment of up to six months for employers who confiscate migrant workers' documents. In response to this decree, thousands of migrant workers from Cambodia, Laos, and Myanmar began heading home, sparking fears of another mass exodus similar to the one in 2014. As a result, the government suspended the provisions of the decree and instead enacted a new one in June 2018 which (1) decreased fines on irregular migrants to 5,000-50,000 baht, (2) decreased fines on employers to 10,000-100,000 baht per unauthorized worker, (3) required workers to inform officials of their employee and workplace within 15 days from the start date and every time they change employers (Grimwade & Neumann, 2019).

These revised provisions have been welcomed by various stakeholders (Harkins, 2019) but many problems remain. Such punitive fines and complex bureaucratic procedures continue to discourage migrant workers from using official channels such as through the MOUs with host countries and regularization through the NV process. Because irregular channels continue to proliferate, labor abuses are rife, especially in the fishing industry. Moreover, the revised decree does not allow registration with multiple employers which fails to take into account the reality of fluctuating employment situations and leaves migrant workers vulnerable when they lose their status by changing employers (Grimwade & Neumann, 2019). The fact that MOUs were originally initiated by the NSC indeed suggests a securitized approach to labor migration with greater emphasis on criminalizing use of informal recruitment channels and penalizing deviations from using formal channels, rather than maximizing labor efficiency and protecting migrant workers' rights.

Two healthcare schemes are currently available to migrant workers, the Social Security Scheme (SSS) which targets documented migrants in the formal sector, and the Migrant Health Insurance Scheme (MHIS) which targets all other migrants including undocumented ones (Moungsookjareoun and Kersetz, 2019). Undocumented migrant workers can register at One Stop

Service Centres (OSSCs) comprised of the Ministry of the Interior issuing temporary identity cards, the Ministry of Labour issuing temporary work permits, and the Ministry of Public Health conducting the medical exam and enrolling migrants in the HICS, with durations of 6 months to one year. Migrant workers must then undergo the NV process at their home country embassy to receive full work permits and identity documents beyond this period (Loganathan, et. al., 2019: 18). Arguably, the NV requirement deters undocumented migrants, particularly refugees and asylum seekers who are unable to receive verification from their home countries. Indeed, Moungsookjareoun and Kersetz (2019) estimate that only 64 percent of migrant workers from Cambodia, Laos, Myanmar, and Vietnam are enrolled in either SSS or MHIS and this figure drops to 51 percent if undocumented migrants are to be included. Without the benefit of health insurance, undocumented workers would have difficulty covering the cost of medical treatment and may instead avoid seeking medical attention altogether.

While the current military government came to power relatively recently, Thailand has had a long legacy of militarism that has profoundly influenced Thai politics. One proof of this is the proliferation of paramilitary organizations throughout the country, and especially along its border regions. Desmond Ball and David Scott Matthieson in a book called *Militia Redux: Or Sor and the Revival of Paramilitarism in Thailand* (2007) write that paramilitary organizations have been a perennial feature of Thai political development since the early 17th century[4] and that "a bewildering array" exist in Thailand (Ball & Matthieson, 2007:1). Many were limited to a particular region or sector of the country while others operated in a single province. A large number have quietly disappeared for one of many reasons: changes in the strategic environment such as the rise and fall of communist and Muslim insurgencies, domestic issues such as public discontent over "eventually unpalatable gross violations of human rights," and/ or the relative influence and support of their bureaucratic sponsors such as the Army or the various departments within the MOI (Ball & Matthieson, 2007:23-24). A large number remain, however, and they serve a multiplicity of functions such as protecting the country's borders from incursions; providing village security in remote areas; promoting nationalism; combating insurgency, especially by the Communist Party of Thailand from 1965 to 1985; providing civil defense capabilities such as disaster relief; protecting hill-tribes, refugees, and other settlers; as well as serving various political and bureaucratic interests (Ball & Matthieson, 2007: 23). Three of the largest paramilitary organizations are the Border Patrol Police (BPP or *Tor Chor*), the Volunteer Defence Corps (VDC

---

[4] Both the Or Sor and the Royal Thai Army's Territorial Defense Department trace their history as far back as the 1590s to a volunteer force that served as forward scouts during King Naresuan victorious battle for Ayutthaya and Lan-Na Kingdoms (Ball & Matthieson, 2007:4).

or *Or Sor*), and the Rangers (*Thahan Phran*).

Because of their presence in border regions, they are often the first Thai officials encountered by any refugee, asylum seeker, or migrant worker traveling through informal channels into Thailand. The fate of refugees are virtually in the hands of these officials who at that point may decide to intimidate, frighten, and take advantage of the refugees; force them back across the border; or allow them to proceed to a refugee camp (Ball & Matthieson, 2007:165). Reputations of the various military and paramilitary groups differ. The 4th Infantry Division in the 3rd Army Region is said to be more flexible while the 9th Infantry Division in the 1st Army Region is considered the harshest and least flexible of the Army Divisions in the Burma border provinces. The 9th Division has been involved in numerous incidents of refoulement including the pushback in March 1997 of some Karen women, children, and elderly men; in January 2003 of eleven Karen villagers including an infant who had been living in Sangkhlaburi District for more than a decade and had possessed Thai identity cards; in January 2005 of about 558 Karen; and numerous other incidents (Ball & Matthieson, 2007:166-167). Meanwhile, some units of the Volunteer Defense Crops (VDC or *Or Sor*) are seen to take more kindly to refugees. Ball & Matthieson take note of one Or Sor checkpoint in Tak province with a sign that reads "To help protect hilltribe people from another country," while Or Sor units in Umphang District say that they "take care of Karen people," and take them to the camp in Nu Pho (Ball & Matthieson, 2007:165). In a number of cases of refoulement, the Or Sor are sometimes seen to be more lenient than other groups. They would sometimes allow asylum seekers to proceed to camps when the Army or other paramilitary forces would not (Ball & Matthieson, 2007:167).

Impact on refugees and asylum seekers

Like Malaysia, Thailand hosted a large number of refugees and asylum seekers during the so-called Indochinese refugee crisis starting in 1975, as well as various ethnic minorities fleeing Myanmar since the 1980s. But due to its proximity and shared borders, the numbers have been much higher and the Thai government has been able to confine them in camps. Between 1975 and 1997, under the CPA, Thailand hosted more than 757,500 Cambodian, Lao, and Vietnamese refugees and asylum seekers, of which some 705,400 were later resettled in third countries (Robinson, 1998). In 1984, some 10,000 ethnic Karen from Myanmar sought refuge from Burmese military offensives in Thailand. As conflict, violence, and oppression of various ethnic minorities continued in Burma, the number of refugees and asylum seekers in Thailand grew. As of July 2018, over 102,000 refugees and asylum seekers were registered with the UNHCR in Thailand. Of these, about 97,500 were ethnic minorities from Myanmar living in 9 camps along the Thai-Myanmar border.

The rest are urban refugees living mainly in Bangkok (APRRN, 2018b).

Like Malaysia, Thailand has no national asylum framework for recognizing refugees and their rights under international law. As a result they are considered 'illegal aliens' under Thailand's immigration laws. Unlike Malaysia, however, Thailand has urban-based refugees, mainly in Bangkok, from countries such as Pakistan, Vietnam, Cambodia, Palestine, Syria, and Somalia, as well as refugees and asylum seekers, mainly ethnic Karen and Karenni, living in nine 'temporary camps' along the border with Myanmar. Refugees and asylum seekers in Bangkok would register with the UNHCR and apply for RSD which, like in Kuala Lumpur, can take a long time. Without any source of income, those refugees and asylum seekers are also forced to work illegally, leaving them vulnerable to exploitation, poor access to welfare, and the constant threat of arbitrary arrest, detention, imprisonment, and deportation. Meanwhile, refugees and asylum seekers in the border camps have been receiving limited assistance such as food and shelter, and later medicine, healthcare, and sanitation, from a consortium of NGOs, administered through respective community organizations since they first arrived in 1984. The UNHCR acquired an operational role and access to border populations only in 1998, on the condition that they are limited to a protection role (rather than providing material assistance), and that they seek durable solutions[5].

Elsewhere I have documented efforts by the UNHCR to register those refugees and seek durable solutions to their plight (Lego, 2018). Universal registration of the border populations began only in 1999 and a mechanism called the Provincial Admissions Boards (PABs), consisting of Thai officials from various branches of government and a representative from the UNHCR, was set up to determine whether an applicant is eligible to remain in Thailand on a temporary basis (UNHCR, 2006). Registration was discontinued at the end of 2001 but was resumed in 2004 during which more than 101,000 persons were re-registered from the 1999 exercise, and another 34,000 were identified. These 135,000 persons registered in 1999 and 2004 became eligible for resettlement. Since 2004, over 139,000 refugees from Thailand have been resettled in 14 different countries (IOM Thailand, 2018). For the 97,000 or so who remain in camps, living conditions remain harsh and there is minimal freedom of movement. Refugees and asylum seekers are technically not allowed to leave the camps for work, but in fact families living in camps often have some connection migrant workers outside towns and it is not uncommon for able-bodied refugees and asylum seekers living in

---

[5] The UNHCR seeks three kinds of so-called durable solutions for refugees—integration, resettlement, or repatriation. Because the Thai government officially denies the possibility of local integration resettlement and repatriation are the only options for refugees and asylum seekers arriving in Thailand.

camps to seek livelihood in nearby border towns.[6] Unfortunately, they do so at great risk given their precarious status.

Due to ceasefire agreements between the Myanmar's military and some of the ethnic groups along the border, efforts to undertake voluntary repatriation have been gaining ground in the last three years. In 2016, 71 refugees returned voluntarily to Myanmar and another 103 also repatriated in the first half of 2018. However, human rights groups continue to raise concerns about ongoing presence of the Burmese military in ethnic regions, active armed conflict in northern Myanmar, reports of human rights violations, continued placement and existence of uncleared landmines, oppressive and discriminatory laws, lack of equal access to citizenship rights, land ownership issues, and unequal access to adequate healthcare, livelihood, and education. Meanwhile, arrest and detention of refugees and asylum seekers continue, including pregnant women and young children, some of whom are separated from their mothers (APRRN, 2018b).

In sum, refugees and asylum seekers arriving in Thailand, much like those arriving in Malaysia, also try to make a living and are drawn to labor opportunities while awaiting a so-called durable solution to their situation. However, both those who live in Bangkok and in camps along the border are faced with hostile immigration policies which (1) criminalize illegal entry and their mere presence on Thai soil, (2) penalize them for making a living, and (3) place them at risk of being returned to the same dangers they were fleeing from in the first place. Those in camps receive limited food, temporary shelter, welfare, and assistance (e.g., health and education) from NGOs but those who are not in camps have even fewer options. Talks of peace in Myanmar may seem promising but the situation of many refugees and asylum seekers in Thailand remain precarious.

Conclusion

Thailand and Malaysia both struggle to manage labor migration as result of a kind of institutional denial of their economies' dependence on low wage labor and a resulting resistance to establishing long term employment options and protection of migrant workers. As a result, there are no comprehensive labor migration frameworks, mechanisms for recruitment are complicated, and provisions to regularize migrant workers' legal status are ad hoc. This in turn leads to large numbers of migrant workers being recruited without the proper documentation or eventually losing their documented status. In one

---

[6] During this author's field work in the border town of Mae Sot in 2013, she had come to learn that Burmese manager of the hostel she was staying at had family inside the nearby camp. She was then given an opportunity to visit this family and see the conditions inside the camp. In conversation with this family, she learned that there were indeed others who either lived in camps or found work in nearby towns while having family living inside the camps.

sense, the large demand for low-cost labor in Thailand and Malaysia provide refugees and asylum seekers the opportunity to work and generate some income despite not being permitted to work on account of their status. However, they are subject to the same harsh penalties as other undocumented migrant workers but without some of the protections those migrant workers may have on account of possessing citizenship from another country. The most glaring of these is that there is nowhere for them to be safely deported to during an immigration crackdown. In the case of Thailand, availing of the NV process would not be an option for them. Consequently, both Thailand and Malaysia are, at the very least, complicit in the exploitation of vulnerable refugees and asylum seekers who have no home state to seek protection from, save the ad hoc intervention of the UNHCR and some NGOs. At worst, in the process of implementing immigration crackdowns and deportations, there have been blatant violations of international customary law with deportations of refugees and asylum seekers tantamount to *refoulement*. While Malaysia has mobilized a significant section of its civilian population through an enthusiastic volunteer corps, Thailand has a host of military and paramilitary resources to ensure these outcomes. The two countries indeed share many similarities, foremost of which is the need acknowledge their dependence on low-wage labor, and the need to view their migrant workers along with their refugees and asylum seekers as living resources to be valued and protected rather than be dispensed of if they are to maintain economic growth at all, and more so if it is to be done humanely.

References

Amnesty International. (2010). *Abused and abandoned: Refugees denied rights in Malaysia.* Available at http://www.amnesty.org/en/library/asset/ASA28/010/2010/en/53561f51-084a-4b9c- 9126-be7c64e8583e/asa280102010ms.pdf, accessed January 10, 2010.

Archavanitkul, K. and Hall, A. (2011). Migrant workers and human rights in Thai context. In J.W. Huguet & A. Chamratrithirong (eds.), *Thailand migration report 2011: Migration for development in Thailand: Overview and tools for policymakers* (pp.63-74). Available at http://publications.iom.int/system/files/pdf/tmr_2011.pdf, accessed 15 January 2016.

Asia Pacific Refugee Rights Network (APRRN). (2018a). Country Fact Sheet: Malaysia. Available at http://aprrn.info/wp-content/uploads/2018/09/APRRN-Country-Factsheet-Malaysia-4-Sept-2018.pdf

APRRN. (2018b). Country Fact Sheet: Thailand. Available at http://aprrn.info/wp-content/uploads/2018/09/APRRN-Country-Factsheet-Thailand-4-Sept-2018.pdf

Ball, D. and Matthieson, D.S. (2007). *Militia redux: Or Sor and the revival of paramilitarism in Thailand.* Bangkok: White Lotus, Co. Ltd.

Batistella, G. (2004). "Migration without borders: A long way to go in the Asian region." In A. Pecoud and P. de Guchteneire (eds.), *Migration without borders: Essays on the free movement of people.* New York & Oxford: Berghahn Books.

Bylander, M. and Reid, G. (2017). "Criminalizing irregular migrant labor: Thailand's crackdown in context." *Migration Information Source.* Migration Policy Institute. Available at https://www.migrationpolicy.org/article/criminalizing-irregular-migrant-labor-thailands-crackdown-context

Chalamwong, Y., Meepien, J. and Hongprayoon, K. (2012). Management of cross-border migration: Thailand as a case of net immigration. *Asian Journal of Social Science* 40: 447-463.

Chantavanich, S. (2007). Thailand policies towards migrant workers from Myanmar. Paper presented at the APMRN Conference at Fujian Normal University, Fuzhou, PRC during 26-28 May 2007.

Derks, A. (2013). "Human rights and (im)mobility: Migrants and the state in Thailand." *Sojourn: Journal of Social Issues in Southeast Asia* 28 (2): 216-240.

Devadason, E.S. and Chan, W. M. (2011). *A critical appraisal of policies and laws regulating migrant workers in Malaysia.* Available at http://www.wbiconpro.com/210-DEVADASON.pdf, accessed 15 January 2016.

Equal Rights Trust (ERT). (2010). *Trapped in a cycle of flight: Stateless Rohingya in Malaysia.* Available at http://www.equalrightstrust.org/ertdocumentbank/ERTMalaysia ReportFinal.pdf accessed December 30, 2010.

Garces-Mascarenas, B. (2015). Revisiting bordering practices: Irregular migration, borders, and citizenship in Malaysia. *International political sociology* 9: 128-142.

Grimwade, M. and Neumann, P. (2019). "Migration policy and practice in Thailand." In B. Harkins (ed.), *Thailand migration report 2019,* Bangkok: United Nations Thematic Working Group on Migration in Thailand.

Hall, A. (2011). Migration and Thailand: Policy, perspectives and challenges. In J. W. Huguet, & A. Chamratrithirong (eds.), *Thailand migration report 2011: Migration for development in Thailand: Overview and tools for policymakers* (pp.17-38). Available at http://publications.iom.int/system/files/pdf/tmr_2011.pdf, accessed 15 January 2016.

Huguet, J.W. and Chamratrithirong, A. (Eds.) (2011). *Thailand migration report 2011: Migration for development in Thailand: Overview and tools for policymakers.* Bangkok: International Migration Office. Available at http://publications.iom.int/system/files/pdf/tmr_2011.pdf, accessed 15 January 2016.

Human Development Social Protection and Labor Unit (HDSPLU). (2013). *Immigration in Malaysia: Assessment of its economic effects and a review of the policy system.* Report completed in collaboration with the ILMIA—Ministry of Human Resources of Malaysia. Document of the World Bank.

Harkins, B. (ed.). (2019). Thailand Migration Report 2019. *Bangkok: United Nations Thematic Working Group on Migration in Thailand.*

Hedman, E. E. (2008). Refuge governmentality and citizenship: Capturing 'illegal migrants' in Malaysia and Thailand. *Government and Opposition* 43 (2): 358-383.

Immigration Act 1959/63 55 (1) (Malaysia). Available at http://www.agc.gov.my/ agcportal/uploads/files/Publications/LOM/EN/Act%20155.pdf

International Federation for Human Rights (FIDH) and Suara Rakyat Malaysia (SUARAM). *Undocumented Migrants and Refugees in Malaysia: Raids, Detention and Discrimination.* March 2008.International Labour Organization (ILO). (2018). International Labour Migration Statistics (ILMS) Database in ASEAN. Available at http://apmigration.ilo.org/asean-labour-migration-statistics

International Organization for Migration (IOM) Mission in Thailand. (2018). IOM Thailand: Refugee Resettlement. Available at https://thailand.iom.int/sites/default/ files/Infosheets/IOM%20Infosheet%20-%20Refugee%20Resettlement.pdf

Kassim, A., Too, T., Wong, S.C.M., and Abidin, M.Z. (2014). The management of foreign workers in Malaysia: Institutions and governance regime. In R.H. Adams & A. Ahsan (eds.), *Managing international migration for development in East Asia* (pp.241-262). Washington, D.C.: World Bank.

Kassim, A. and Zin, R. H.M. (2011). Policy on irregular migrants in Malaysia. An analysis of its implementation and effectiveness. *Discussion Paper Series* No. 2011-34. Philippine

Institute for Development Studies.

Kassim, A. (1987). "The unwelcome guests: Indonesian immigrants and Malaysian public responses." *Southeast Asian Studies* 25 (2): 265-278.

Kaur, A. (2008). International migration and governance in Malaysia: Policy and performance. *UNEAC Asia Papers* 22. Available at http://www.une.edu.au/ asiacentre/PDF/No22.pdf, accessed 15 November 2010.

Lee, H., and Khor, L. Y. (2018). "Counting migrant workers in Malaysia: A needlessly persisting conundrum." *ISEAS Yusof Ishak Institute Perspective*, *25*. Available at https://www.iseas.edu.sg/images/pdf/ISEAS_Perspective_2018_25@50.pdf

Lego, J. (2012). "Protecting and Assisting Refugees and Asylum-Seekers in Malaysia: The Role of the UNHCR, Informal Mechanisms, and the 'Humanitarian Exception". *Journal of Political Science & Sociology*, (17): 75-99.

Lego, J. (2018). "Making refugees (dis) appear: Identifying refugees and asylum seekers in Thailand and Malaysia." *Austrian Journal of South-East Asian Studies*, *11*(2), 183-198.

Loganathan, et. al. (2019). "Breaking down the barriers: Understanding migrant workers' access to healthcare in Malaysia". *PLoS ONE* 14(7): e0218669. https://doi.org/ 10.1371/journal.pone.0218669

Moungsookjareoun, A. and Kersetz, D. (2019). Towards universal health coverage for migrants in Thailand. In B. Harkins (ed.), *Thailand migration report 2019,* Bangkok: United Nations Thematic Working Group on Migration in Thailand.

Nadaraj, V. (2013). Reinventing RELA: Malaysia's volunteer corps moving with the times. *The Establishment Post.* Available at http://www.establishmentpost.com/reinventing-rela-malaysias-volunteer-corps-moving-times/ accessed 4 January 2016.

Nah, A. M. (2012). Globalisation, sovereignty and immigration control: The hierarchy of rights for migrant workers in Malaysia. *Asian Journal of Social Science* 40: 486-508.

Nah, A. (2007). Struggling with (il)legality: The indeterminate functioning of Malaysia's borders for asylum seekers, refugees, and stateless persons. In P.K. Rajaram & C. Grundy-Warr (eds.), *Borderscapes: Hidden geographies and politics at territory's edge* (pp. 33-64). Minneapolis: University of Minnesota Press.

Pillai, P. (1999). "The Malaysian state's responses to migration." *Sojourn* 14 (1): 178-197.

Robinson, C.W. (1998). *Terms of refuge: The Indochinese exodus and the international response.* London: Zed Books.

Smith, H., Lim, R., and Harkins, B. (2019). Thailand Migration Profile. In B. Harkins (ed.), *Thailand migration report 2019,* Bangkok: United Nations Thematic Working Group on Migration in Thailand.

Thai PBS. (2015). Deadline for nationality verification of foreign migrant workers extended until June 29. Available at http://englishnews.thaipbs.or.th/content/10204 7, accesed 15 January 2016.

Thailand Law Forum. (2009). Alien Working Act, B.E., 2551. Available at http://www.thailawforum.com/database1/Alien-Working-Act.html, accessed 15 January 2016.

The Malaysia Insider. (2013, January 31). Claiming foreign worker levy a discrimination, MTUC to complain to ILO. Available at http://www.themalaysianinsider.com/ malaysia/article/claiming-foreign-worker-levy-a- discrimination-mtuc-to-complain-to-ilo accessed 3 January 2016

Thaweesit, S. and Napaumporn, B. (2011). Integration of minorities in Thailand. In J.W. Huguet & A. Chamratrithirong (eds.), *Thailand migration report 2011: Migration for development in Thailand: Overview and tools for policymakers* (pp.131-144). Available at http://publications.iom.int/system/files/pdf/tmr_2011.pdf, accessed 15 January 2016.

United Nations High Commissioner for Refugees (UNHCR). (2006). Analysis of Gaps in Refugee Protection Capacity. Available at https://www.unhcr.org/457ed0412.pdf

UNHCR Malaysia. (2020). Figures at a glance. Available at https://www.unhcr.org/figures-at-a-glance-in-malaysia.html

Wong, D. (2002). The national context of migration research in Malaysia: Which nation? What state? Whose migration? In M. Bommes & D. Thranhardt (eds.), *National paradigms of migration research* (pp. 301-314). Osnabruck: V&R Unipress.

World Bank. (2019). Malaysia: Estimating the number of foreign workers. © World Bank. Available at

CHAPTER 3

THE JAPANESE ASYLUM POLICIES: THE INFORMAL ASYLUM OF SYRIANS IN JAPAN

Yahya Almasri

Introduction

The Syrian conflict has caused a massive death toll, destruction, and one of the largest displacement crises since World War II. Since the outbreak of the war, a decade ago, millions of Syrians have embarked on desperate journeys in the hope of restarting their lives in safety. Approximately 6.6 million Syrians escaped the horrors of war fleeing to neighboring countries; 6.1 million became internally displaced, which is more than half of Syria's population, estimated at 22 million in 2010 (UNHCR 2020). Hundreds of Syrians have settled in Japan, a country with a rigid refugee system that effectively deters both fake and genuine asylum seekers. The refugee recognition rate in Japan has not exceeded 1% since 2011 (Japan Lawyer Network for Refugees 2020). Whether or not it was an informed decision for Syrians to seek protection in the East Asian archipelago, most of them have not applied for refugee status.

Instead, they preferred to maintain their temporary visas issued by the Japanese Ministry of Justice as a form of informal asylum. Why do the majority of Syrian asylum seekers in Japan opt for the informal asylum, and what are its consequences? To answer these questions, I will first trace the historical development of the Japanese asylum policies and analyze the main reasons that make it a subject of controversy. Second, I will explain the treatment of Syrian asylum seekers, or "the Syria case, " and the informal asylum consequences.

Japan generously placed itself as one of the major donors to the humanitarian needs of Syrian refugees since 2012. The humanitarian aid from Japan was estimated to be more than 2.7 billion US dollars by the end of 2019 (Diplomatic Blue Book 2020, 149). Tokyo is not directly involved in the Syrian war, reiterating that "Japan has consistently maintained a stance that the crisis in Syria cannot be resolved by any military means," stating that "a political solution is indispensable." (Diplomatic Blue Book 2020, 149) Unlike oil-producing countries in the Middle East, the history of mutual bonds does not suggest strategic interests nor does it have deep cultural ties. For the majority of Syrians, Japan is a very unusual travel destination, but the country enjoys a positive and apolitical image among them. Contrary to Eastern and

South-Eastern Asian countries, Japan did not leave any imperial legacy or historical disputes with Syria.

Methodology

This is the first empirical study of Syrian asylum seekers in Japan that involves primary and secondary sources. Thirty-one semi-structured interviews with Syrian asylum seekers, Japanese NGO directors, and refugee lawyers in the Kansai and Kanto regions were conducted. In addition to fieldwork, I assisted refugee lawyers and NGOs with their work with asylum seekers between 2015 and 2020. The first-hand experience deepened my understanding of asylum and migration issues in the country. My usage of the term "informal asylum" is inspired by Gibney's (2008) article that elaborates on the survival strategies of asylum seekers in the UK coping with deportations and rejections of asylum applications under the government of the then- British prime minister Tony Blair in 2006. Gibney wrote: "An asylum seeker may opt for a kind of 'informal asylum', outside the purview of the state, because they do not trust state officials to make fair or accurate decisions on refugee status." (Gibney 2008,151) The purpose of this study is not to compare the Japanese asylum policies with the British ones. Nevertheless, Gibney's term best applies to the Syrian asylum seekers case in Japan. There is a further explanation of the situation below.

The Development of the Japanese Asylum Policies

In recent years, the number of refugee applications has significantly increased, whereas refugee's recognition rate has dropped to an unprecedented level, as shown in the table below.

Table 3.1. Asylum applications and refugee recognition in Japan

Year	Number of Refugee Applicants	Number of Recognized Refugees	Refugee Recognition Rate
2000	216	22	13.8%
2010	1,202	39	1.9%
2011	1,867	21	0.3%
2012	2,545	18	0.2%
2013	3,260	6	0.1%
2014	5,000	11	0.2%
2015	7,686	27	0.6%
2016	10,901	28	0.3%
2017	19,628	20	0.2%
2018	10,494	42	0.4%
2019	10,375	44	0.9%

Retrieved from Japan Lawyers Network for Refugees, 2020.

Prior to accession to the 1951 UN Refugee Convention and its 1967

Protocol in 1981, Japan was a stopover for asylum seekers who wished to reach Western countries, mainly the United States. For instance, a Soviet pilot landed his Mig-25 fighter jet in Hakodate Airport in Hokkaido in 1976 to announce his defection in the neighboring US ally. The pilot was arrested and charged with six crimes against Japan. The crimes were mainly related to illegal entry. The pilot prepared himself for deportation afterward. But since he expressed his desire to seek asylum in the United States "via Japan", he was granted asylum in the United States in a matter of four days (Takeda 1998, 436).

In fact, there are many similar incidents where Japan either deported asylum seekers such as in the case of the Taiwanese political leader Liu Yu Jun in 1968, or Japan requested the help of western countries to accept them as refugees. (Arakaki 2016,13) In a nutshell, there was no asylum policy nor refugee law that provided asylum seekers with protection or guaranteed them their fundamental human rights in Japan. (Arakaki 2016,15) In 1979, the government of Japan inaugurated a "Refugee Affairs Headquarters" known now as the "Refugee Assistance Headquarters" RHQ as a part of the "Foundation for Welfare and Education for Asia Orphans" in view of improving the conditions of asylum seekers in Japan (Mukae 2001,133).

The arrival of Indochinese refugees known in Japan as "boat people" combined with intense international pressure pushed the then-Japanese government to ratify the 1951 Refugee Convention and its 1967 Protocol in 1981, thirty years after it was adopted. Although Japan was a latecomer to the international refugee system, it was the first East Asian country that signed the Convention. The Japanese Ministry of Justice (MOJ) took the sole responsibility for implementing the Convention after the revision of the Immigration Control and Refugee Recognition Act in early 1982. (Honma 2008, 24)This crucial decision paved the way for refugees and foreign residents like *Zainichi* Koreans, who experienced social and legal discrimination, to gain legal rights (Mukae 2001,150).

Japan's heavy reliance on oil imports from the Middle East as well as its domestic labor shortage, both influenced its policy toward Iranian asylum seekers. Thousands of Iranians who fled the Khomeini regime in the early 1980s were allowed to stay and work in Japan without granting them refugee status. Tokyo improved its relations with the Gulf states after the 1973 oil crisis and signed a bilateral visa-exempt agreement with Iran. (Sellek 2001,48) As a result, a visa-free Japan sounded like an alluring destination for Iranian asylum seekers. The number of Iranian asylum seekers or "illegal workers" was estimated by 37,457 in 1992. Japan decided to freeze the agreement in the same year to restrict the entry of Iranians (Morita 2003,159-160).

The 1990 Immigration Control and Refugees Recognition Act was another crucial legal development. The Act increased the number of foreign residents' residence statuses in Japan from eighteen to twenty-seven. To deal with the labor shortage at that time, the Act permitted the entry of the third-generation Japanese descendants in Brazil and Peru (*nikkeijin*), without restricting their activities while residing in Japan. (Brody 2002,41) However, the ban on unskilled foreign labor was not lifted. Consequently, asylum seekers who applied for refugee status were unable to access the labor market freely. Lucky ones undertook underpaid and undignifying jobs domestically known as "3K jobs" (dirty, dangerous, and demeaning in Japanese) away from the authorities' eyes.

Tourist visa requirements were relaxed for many Asian countries to boost inbound tourism. But the relaxation led to a surge of refugee applications in recent years. The number of refugee applicants reached 19,629 in 2017, which is the highest ever in Japan's history. To cope with the new phenomenon, the MOJ started to implement a new revision on the Japanese refugee system from January 2018 to prevent false asylum seekers from exploiting the refugee system. The revision classifies refugee applicants into four main categories:

A: Applicants with a high possibility of facing persecution due to war under the 1951 Refugee Convention.

B: Applicants who are not facing persecution under the Refugee Convention, such as those stating personal reasons like debt or inheritance troubles.

C: Applicants who were rejected before and re-applied or appealed based on invalid grounds.

D: Those who do not fall under category A, B, and C. (The Japanese Ministry of Justice and Japan Association for Refugees 2018)

The new revision caused a significant decrease in the number of refugee applications for the first time since 2010, from 19,629 applications in 2017 to 10,493 in 2018. However, it did not reform the refugee policy itself.

Immigration and asylum policies are inseparable. The former has been a taboo topic in Japan, but the acute labor shortage and aging population pushed the Japanese parliament to pass a major immigration bill in December 2018 to attract 345,000 "semi-skilled" foreign workers. (Denyer and Kashiwagi 2018) The policy shift was met with fierce opposition by many conservative parties. They argued that relaxing the immigration policy would depress wages and exploit the national health system by foreign workers' families. They also warned that immigrants would take jobs away from Japanese nationals, undermine social cohesion, and threaten public safety. (The Mainichi 2018) Shinzo Abe, the former Prime Minister of Japan, justified the market-led decision. He calmed the nerves of his rivals and support base alike by stating that "This is not an immigration policy." (Sugiyama 2018). Public polls indicate more tolerant views of the bill. The October 2018 Nikkei survey showed that 54% of the Japanese public were in favor of the bill (Ebuchi and Takeuchi 2018). The November 2018 Kyodo News poll put it at 51.3 % (the Japan Times 2018), and NHK at 27% approve, 30% disapprove and 36% undecided. Japan will need to fill 6.4 million jobs by 2030 (Kamata 2018). But rampant exploitation at workplaces led some foreign workers to commit suicide, while another 9,052 went missing. The Japanese Ministry of Justice took countermeasures to curb the phenomenon (Osumi 2019).

Two Main Reasons for the Controversial Asylum Policies in Japan

The 2015 "refugee crisis" reignited debates on Japan's asylum policies and questioned its unwillingness to participate in the burden-sharing process. The following are the two main reasons for Japan's controversial asylum policy:

First, weak political will to resettle refugees in Japan. Scholar Ryuji Mukea evaluated the generous Japanese donations to the international refugee regime, but he accurately predicted in 2001 that Japan would keep facing international criticism for not resettling refugees.

He explains:

"It is no exaggeration to say that without Japanese funding the refugee regime will be unable to sustain itself for long. This remains to be true regardless of Japan's motives for such financial generosity. Nevertheless, as long as Tokyo uses its financial power to "compensate" for its own poor resettlement record, such a stance will continue to be criticized internationally simply because refugee-intake is yet another component of international burden-sharing." (Mukae 2001, 238).

During the peak of the 2015 refugee crisis, Shinzo Abe made it very clear that Japan would not accept refugees at the UN General Assembly in September 2015. "I would say that before accepting immigrants or refugees, we need to have more activities by women, elderly people and we must raise our birth rate. There are many things that we should do before accepting immigrants," Abe said (Reuters 2015).

The vast majority of Japanese politicians tend to remain silent about refugees. In 2011, both houses of the Japanese Diet adopted "the world's first" resolution regarding the protection of refugees in commemoration of the 30th anniversary of Japan becoming a party to the 1953 Refugee Convention. But the resolution did not have any impact on increasing acceptance of refugees or guided the action of Diet members towards reforming the asylum policy itself (Takizawa 2018,7).

The dominating political elite in Japan leaves refugee NGOs with limited wiggle room. Mieko Ishikawa, Director of the International Social Services Japan (ISSJ), highlights the challenging environment for her advocacy work. She explains:

"The few pro-refugee parliamentarians are members of Japanese opposition parties that have no major influence over decision-making. If we (refugee NGOs) ask people in Shaminto (SocialDemocratic Party) or Komeito to adopt our cause, then we will end up in a conflict with the ruling party (LDP) without benefiting refugees. So we have no other option but to keep trying with those in the LDP. Many NGOs in Japan take the anti-government style in their advocacy work. I think we all have to follow another strategy".(personal communication, March 27, 2019)

It is wrong to assume that the LDP-run government in Tokyo is not taking the refugee issue seriously. At the same time, it is not in the process of bringing about a major policy reform yet. NGOs/NPOs in Japan hold two meetings a year with the Japanese Ministry of Justice, and one with the Ministry of Foreign Affairs.

Ishikawa remarks:

"These meetings are not intended to change the refugee policy itself. We (NGOs) only share information and exchange opinions with policymakers on issues related to refugees or foreign residents." Forum for Refugees Japan (FRJ) plays a leading role in representing its 21 refugee organizations and conveying their requests and proposals to policymakers (personal communication, March 27, 2019)

On the other hand, the Japanese Ministry of Justice (MOJ) explained in a press release in 2018 that the majority of applicants for refugee recognition are "originating" from countries where there are "no circumstances causing a mass exodus of refugees / displaced persons". Therefore, Japan has a meager rate of refugee recognition regardless of the political will to resettle refugees or increase its low refugee recognition record.

"The few pro-refugee parliamentarians are members of Japanese opposition parties that have no major influence over decision-making. If we (refugee NGOs) ask people in Shaminto (SocialDemocratic Party) or Komeito to adopt our cause, then we will end up in a conflict with the ruling party (LDP) without benefiting refugees. So we have no other option but to keep trying with those in the LDP. Many NGOs in Japan take the anti-government style in their advocacy work. I think we all have to follow another strategy". (personal communication, March 27, 2019)

Table 3.2. Refugee claims in Japan, 2015-2017

	2015		2016		2017	
1	Nepal	1,768	Indonesia	1,829	Philippines	4,895
2	Indonesia	969	Nepal	1,451	Vietnam	3,116
3	Turkey	926	Philippines	1,412	Sri Lanka	2,226
4	Myanmar	808	Turkey	1,143	Indonesia	2,038
5	Vietnam	574	Vietnam	1,072	Nepal	1,451
6	Sri Lanka	469	Sri Lanka	938	Turkey	1,195
7	Philippines	299	Myanmar	650	Myanmar	962
8	Pakistan	295	India	470	Cambodia	772
9	Bangladesh	244	Cambodia	318	India	601
10	India	229	Pakistan	289	Pakistan	469
11	China	167	Bangladesh	242	Bangladesh	438
12	Nigeria	154	Ghana	174	China	315
13	Thailand	83	China	156	Iran	120
14	Iran	68	Nigeria	108	Ghana	106
15	Cameroon	67	Iran	107	Cameroon	98
16	Cambodia	67	Cameroon	66	Tunisia	87
17	Ghana	50	Tunisia	63	Nigeria	77
18	Uganda	42	Senegal	45	Senegal	75
19	Tunisia	32	Uganda	39	Uganda	68
20	DR of the Congo	24	DR of the Congo	39	Thailand	65
21	Senegal	23	Guinea	38	Mongolia	61
22	Ukraine	20	Egypt	31	DR of the Congo	35
23	Ethiopia	17	Mongolia	29	Guinea	26
24	Guinea	16	Thailand	21	Egypt	24
25	Egypt	14	Ethiopia	13	Ethiopia	22
—	Others	161	Others	158	Others	287
	7,586		**10,901**		**19,629**	

Source: The Japanese Ministry of Justice, 2018.

According to the MOJ, the majority of refugee claims are not related to wars or armed conflicts. For instance, in 2017, 48% of the unrecognized refugee applicants claimed personal troubles like issues with neighbors or criminal elements, 22% applied for refugee status because of their engagement in opposition parties or anti-government activities, 6% due to religious reasons, 5 % due to race, 5% due to troubles with relatives over inheritance, and 5% due to fragile security status in their home countries. (The Japanese Ministry of Justice and Japan Association for Refugees 2018)

The second reason for the controversial asylum policy concerns public attitudes to refugee resettlement. The public has little awareness of human rights in general, and refugee issues in particular. Therefore, the restrictive asylum policies in Japan are a reflection of the public's disinterest and their unsympathetic attitude. (Honma 2008, 23) Ishikawa comments from her experience:

> "The concept of human rights in our society has a strong political image. In general, Japanese people are unwilling to speak about refugees or discrimination issues against minorities like Chinese or Korean residents, Burakumin (an outcast minority group), and Ainu (indigenous ethnic group)." (personal communication, March 27, 2019)

Analyzing public opinion polls on refugees draws a more precise conclusion. The Prime Minister's Office of Japan conducted five public opinion polls about refugees between 1980 to 1995. The first one was about the Indo-Chinese refugees (those who fled Cambodia and Vietnam from the mid-1975s) in May 1980. It shows that 69% of the 2400 respondents said that Japan should offer financial assistance to refugees,18% favored sending Japanese medical teams to a host country of refugees, but only 3% said that Japan should resettle them in Japan. (Takeda 1998, 436)

The Japanese government expanded the intake quota of the Indo-Chinese refugee refugees to 3,000 in April 1982, 5,000 in November 1983, and 10,000 in July 1985. The perception towards refugees considerably improved in the June 1982 poll when respondents were asked: "To what extent should Japan expand its intake quota in the future?". The question was followed by a statistical chart displaying that Japan accepted the lowest number of Indo-Chinese refugee refugees among the United States, Canada, France, Australia, West Germany, and the United Kingdom. 43% of respondents answered that Japan should increase the quota to a certain extent, 29% opposed any increase, 7% wanted a significant increase. (Takeda 1998, 446- 447)

The conservative attitude of the Japanese public towards resettling refugees also applies to Syrian refugees. The Japanese public also opposed accepting refugees from Syria as elsewhere, according to a public opinion poll conducted by the left-leaning Asahi Newspaper in December 2015. The poll indicates that 58% of respondents are against the resettlement of refugees in Japan, while only 24% think that Japan should better accept refugees. (Asahi Shinbun 2016) The February 2017 poll by Mainichi Newspapers about the surge in refugee applications in Japan is not favorable either. 69% of respondents said that "Japan should be cautious about accepting refugees", whereas only 15% believe that Japan should accept refugees. (The Mainichi 2016)

Unlike the case in immigration and refugee-friendly countries, Japan's geographic proximity to Syria and its non-vital interest in the country, the lack of cultural bonds between the two countries, as well as Japan's non-involvement in the Syrian conflict, and in particular security concerns are all factors that negatively influence the Japanese public opinion towards resettling refugees from Syria. Furthermore, home-grown terrorist attacks in European countries such as the November 2015 attack in Paris, and the subsequent scapegoating of refugees in Europe have informed public opinion in Japan. Kaoru Yamaguchi, who previously worked as a Campaign Coordinator for Refugees at Amnesty International Japan, and currently works for Japanese politician Mizuho Fukushima, argues that propagating refugee acceptance in Japan clashes with the mainstream insular mindset, and the public prefers sending ODA instead of creating resettlement schemes. She says:

> "The public thinks it is weird and unpatriotic to talk about benefiting non-Japanese citizens in Japan. That is why the mass majority of Japanese politicians would not express support for accepting refugees. I noticed that Japanese people think that ODA is the best form of assistance for foreigners in their countries not resettling them in Japan out of fear they would commit crimes". (personal communication, March 29, 2019)

Public, as well as, official responses to the plight of refugees in 2015 vary in Japan from those in Western Europe as a senior executive director of a Tokyo-based refugee-support NPO elucidates:

> "From our daily interactions with the public over the past two decades, young Japanese are not interested in refugee issues and seniors express harsh attitudes towards outsiders. The vast majority of Japanese people showed little reaction to the sad images of the Syrian toddler in September 2015. We (the Japanese public) think that the crises of the Middle East are none of our business. We need to mull over of the way Obama and David Cameron announced resettlement programs of Syrians in their countries despite anti-immigrant sentiments. The Japanese government did not do the same". (personal communication. March 24, 2019)

Professor Robert Ford, who is an expert on party politics and public opinion at the University of Manchester, clearly delineates how the British public reacted to the Syrian refugee crisis in the UK to demand their government to resettle refugees in the UK:

> "The reaction to Alan Alkurdi's image is something I have never seen before in this country. All of the newspapers that traditionally demonize refugees were all the sudden clamoring to help refugees.

They completely caught the government off guard. The Daily Mail and the Sun were saying, "how dare you not help these people?!" . (personal communication, March 3, 2018)

Ford suggests that the September 2015 Syrian Vulnerable Person Resettlement Programme is a smart move from Cameron's government to respond to the public without taking in the same number of refugees as Germany did. He comments:

"Our government made the gamble by making a commitment that sounds very big in a headline. They said that the UK would resettle 20,000 refugees from Syria, but they will stretch it out in five years. The public attention will move on to something else, and the UK will not allow the same number of refugees as Germany. This strategy is paying off so far". (personal communication, March 3, 2018).

Table 3.3. Recognized Refugees in selected countries

By the End of 2018	Number of Recognized Applicants	Refugee Recognition Rate
Canada	16,875	56.4%
The United States	35,198	35.4%
The United Kingdom	12,027	32.5%
Germany	56,583	23%
France	29,035	19.2%
Italy	6,448	6.8%
South Korea	118	3.1%
Japan	40	0.3%

Back in Japan, the negative public opinion on refugees is psychological and originates from the lack of contact between Japanese people and refugees. The Japanese public is under-informed about mass displacement, and some NPOs are attempting to address the issue. For instance, WELgee in Tokyo distributes free comic books (manga) that depict the lives of people escaping war zones, including Syrians. WELgee founder Sayaka Watanabe explains:

"Many people have not met refugees before and it is hard for them to imagine their displacement experience. Through manga, we are trying to inform the public that Syrians and others are normal people searching for safety in Japan". (personal communication, March 26, 2019).

In addition to job matching services, her NPO organizes exchange events where Japanese people have the chance to meet refugees\asylum seekers.

Hitoshige Takegaki, Director of Rafiq, an NPO in Osaka, explains that awareness about refugees in Japan is still shallow even after the 2015 refugee crisis. He remarks:

> "The annual World Refugee Day event in Osaka, the largest in the Kansai region of more than 22 million people, barely attracts 100 attendees. This is very disappointing for us." (personal communication, March 25, 2019)

It is worth stressing that Japan has the lowest refugee recognition rate among its G7 peers, even lower than its neighbor, South Korea.

"The Syria Case" or "the Exception" at Japanese Immigration Bureaus

Syrian asylum seekers in the G7 countries are among the most recognized applicants. Italy has the second-lowest recognition rate in the G7 but has granted refugee status to 97% of Syrian asylum applicants in 2018. Syrians' recognition rate stands at 92.7 % in the United Kingdom, the highest among all nationalities. Germany hosted more than 746,000 Syrians by the end of 2018 and granted refugee status to 50.7 % of its Syrian applicants, the highest among other nationalities in the same year. (AIDA 2019)

Before the Syrian war, 150 Syrians were registered as residents of Japan in July, 2010 (Embassy of Japan in Syria 2012). The number of Syrians reached 946 individuals, 68% of them are males (644 male and female 302) as of December of 2019. Hyogo Prefecture hosts 156 Syrians, Tokyo 117, and Osaka 84 (Japanese Government Statistics 2020).81 Syrians applied for refugee status in Japan between 2011 and mid-2017; only 15 applicants were recognized as refugees. The recognition rate stood at 18.51%, which is the lowest for Syrians among the G7 (JAR 2017). The MOJ statistics do not disclose the exact number of those who applied for the informal asylum, but an approximation of 200 people can be estimated so far.

"The Syria Case or "the (Syrian) exception" are interchangeable expressions used among officers of immigration bureaus and refugee-support NGOs referring to the informal asylum of Syrian asylum seekers in Japan (*Shiria kesu, tokurei*). There is no written policy or a particular legal framework known to the public that regulates processing Syrian asylum seekers. But the "Syria Case" is a policy that has been in practice at immigration bureaus nationwide even before the 2018 revision of the refugee system. The policy enables Syrian asylum seekers to receive a renewable visa called "*tokutei katsudo*" or "Designated Activities Visa" with a work permit valid for six months or one year after their temporary visas expire (usually a visitor visa). The DA visa is one of the twenty-seven types of visas issued by the MOJ for foreigners to engage in miscellaneous and short-term activities such as working holiday or job hunting.

The Japanese Ministry of Justice created "the Syria case" as a form of informal asylum that grants Syrian asylum seekers the right to live and work temporarily in Japan as an alternative to resettlement and refugee status. At the same time, Syrians opt for the informal asylum instead of applying for refugee status for many reasons:

First, officers at immigration bureaus nationwide encourage them to apply for informal asylum, as many have reported in the Kanto and Kansai regions. When a Syrian family of three wanted to apply for refugee status before their visitor visas expired, the immigration authorities did not permit them to apply directly. They extended their visitor visas three times and directed the father to apply for informal asylum with the prospect of obtaining a one-year visa and work permit. An NGO strongly advised the family to revisit the immigration bureau and insist on applying for refugee status only. (personal communication with a Syrian family, January 2019)

Second, single young men and family supporters choose the informal asylum since it gives them rapid access to the labor market, where there is a chronic labor shortage and plenty of employment opportunities. This sense of urgency to earn money soon after arrival in Japan comes from the dire financial need to help their families in Syria or its neighboring countries, as well as from the fact that obtaining refugee status in Japan is almost unattainable.[1]

"My children and wife will starve to death if I don't send them money monthly. My garage and house were destroyed in 2012 and we had to rent a small flat in one of Damascus suburbs." (personal communication with a Syrian asylum seeker, May 12, 2018)

Working illegally or "in the black market" could result in deportation or prison. Those who apply for refugee status must rely on the financial assistance of the Refugee Assistance Headquarters (RHQ) to survive because they are not given work permits in the first three to six months of processing their applications. After a rigorous financial assessment, the RHQ only supports the most impoverished asylum seekers for up to four months. An adult can get 1,600 yen as a daily allowance and a maximum of 40,000 yen per month for rent (the Refugee Assistance Headquarters).

In contrast, most asylum seekers of other nationalities are not given job permits easily. Thus, Syrians are treated preferentially in this regard as Hitoshige Takegaki comments:

---

[1]Some Men also arrive in Japan immersed in debt from visa brokers, or from those who helped them to flee Syria.

"Syrian asylum seekers are privileged compared to others because they can receive the Designated Activities visa and work directly without the need to apply for refugee status. The logic of the MOJ is that let them live here temporarily, shop and buy products, pay taxes, and return to their homeland soon after the war ends. But they could stay in Japan for several years." (personal communication, March 25, 2019)

The third reason for opting for the informal asylum is that the procedure of the DA Visa is much smoother and quicker than the regular refugee status procedures. When visiting immigration bureaus, applicants are given a one-page form to state convincing reasons that prevent them from returning home after their temporary visas expire. It takes from two to four weeks for a DA visa to be issued, and applicants are notified with a postcard to collect their visas. In comparison, applicants for formal asylum must fill out a twelve-page form, namely "Application for Recognition of Refugee Status."The entire process is arduous yet time-consuming. Immigration officers demand compelling proof of prosecution and could conduct multiple lengthy interviews with applicants that could last for 10 hours. Commonly, applicants seek assistance from volunteers and refugee support groups to help them articulate their asylum claims in Japanese. The result of the asylum claim can take up to six months.

Fourth, the legal practices of the MOJ are deterring Syrians from applying for refugee status. For legal experts, the MOJ is not fully complying with the 1951 Convention. Equally problematic, the concept of "persecution" is widely misunderstood among Japanese judges, Refugee Examination Councillors (RECs) and inspectors at Immigration Bureaus. In Japan, persecution means "attack or oppression which brings about pain intolerable for ordinary people, which normally signifies violation or suppression of life or freedom of the body". In contrast, in Article 9 of the EU Qualification Directive, for example, "persecution" means "sufficiently serious act by its nature or repetition as to constitute a severe violation of basic human rights". (Hashimoto 2018) The RECs are not fully independent from the Ministry of Justice and the overall restrictive refugee policies drawn by the government. The 90 counselors are not sufficiently trained to handle refugee cases, and their opinions are not legally binding. (Hashimoto 2018)

The MOJ rejected the refugee claims of four Syrian asylum seekers even after they filed a lawsuit against the government at the Tokyo District Court in 2015. Two of the plaintiffs chose to leave Japan to reunite with their families in Europe. The MOJ stated the reasons for rejection:

"Although it cannot be denied that there is the danger of being attacked during the demonstrations, it is a problem that is shared by all people who participate in demonstrations of that kind, and is not a danger that is unique to the appealing party." (Tanaka, 2018)

According to the Syrian constitution, Syrian males between the age of 18 and 42 must serve in the military. The MOJ rejected refugee status application of a draft evader in his early twenties, who claimed that he fled Syria to Japan because he did not want to engage in killing or get killed in battles. The draft evader stated that the Syrian security forces could arrest or retaliate against him if he returned to Syria, but the MOJ rejected his refugee claim. The rejection sheet reads:

> "According to relevant documents, evading the military service in Syria is subject to punishment, but it is not discriminately applied to you. It is generally applied to those who evade the military service, and you can get exempted from the military services by paying exemption fees." (court verdict, 2020).

Conversely, draft evasion in Syria is a valid reason for refugee recognition in 24 European states (The European Commission, 2018). Refugee status applicants are required to submit convincing proof of personal persecution or a high likelihood of being targeted upon return to their homelands. Otherwise, refugee claims would be rejected. Shogo Watanabe, who is a veteran refugee lawyer and the Chief of the Japan Lawyers Network for Refugees, comments on this practice:

> "There is no government in the world that issues a certificate of persecution to its citizens! Judges of the Ministry of Justice should carefully consider the cases of refugee applicants, even without proof. It is disappointing that they (judges) treat refugee cases in the same fashion of general civil law where proof is very crucial. They are not trained in refugee law itself in the first place". (personal communication, April 25, 2019)

Is there an unspoken pressure on judges not to grant refugee status to Syrians or their likes?

Watanabe, the lawyer, thinks otherwise:

> "I think there is no systematic pressure on judges. District Court judges carefully observe the attitude of their superiors at the Supreme Court who are selected by the Prime Minister. This is "Sontaku" (Sontaku is a Japanese word which means a tendency to appease superiors and avoid upsetting them by making decisions that would invoke their disapproval)." He continues: "The current administration is unwilling to assist refugees in Japan and judges cannot swim against the tide." (personal communication, April 25, 2019).

Positive and Negative Consequences of the Informal Asylum:

In reality, the majority of informal asylum seekers from Syria are unintegrated temporary workers. They are mainly males in their early 20s to late 40s; most of them live in shared houses in remote rural areas provided by their employers. Such accommodation not only increases their social exclusion from society but also deepens their dependence on fellow immigrant employers. Unlike recognized refugees who have social benefits and take part in integration programs, they are not eligible to attend the free-of-charge RHQ Japanese language courses since they are not officially recognized as refugees. The mass majority of informal asylum seekers do not speak sufficient Japanese even for basic daily interactions. The language barrier is one of the primary hurdles to integration into Japanese society. Such difficulties motivated the Syrian businessman Abdulkader Homsi to do something for his fellow countrymen in the Kansai region. He established an NPO in June 2016 that provided legal, medical, and Japanese language services. The NPO collapsed after a year and a half due to technical difficulties. (personal communication. September 16, 2018)

The UNHCR defines the self-reliance of refugees as: "Self-reliance is the social and economic ability of an individual, a household or a community to meet essential needs (including protection, food, water, shelter, personal safety, health and education) in a sustainable manner and with dignity." (UNHCR 2005, 1) Syrians achieved significant economic independence thanks to the informal asylum that granted them rapid access to the labor market. The mass majority of them work for car dealers who export second-hand vehicles from Japan to foreign countries. Some workers managed to make decent amounts of savings, as a Syrian paint technician reported 13,000 USD as his annual saving. (personal communication. November 9, 2019)

Labor exploitation and abuse are rampant in workplaces. For example, a Syrian employer confiscated a young man's passport and forced him to work in slavery-like conditions for only $300 a month. (personal communication with two asylum seekers, July 2018) Another Syrian man injured himself seriously while working in a factory and his Japanese employer did not compensate him for a lifetime disability or cover the medical expenses. (personal communication with a Syrian asylum seeker, June 2, 2020). The scarcity of information in Arabic and social support networks led to numerous problems where these workers do not know their rights or duties with regard to their employment.

An informal asylum seeker cannot possess a Japanese "Refugee Travel Document" as the case for recognized refugees. Furthermore, married men suffer from family separation and cannot bring their families to Japan since they are not officially recognized as refugees. One family man exemplifies theses feelings when he states:

> "I fled terror and tyranny in Syria to provide a better life for my wife and sons abroad. I cannot return to Syria or meet them in Japan". (personal communication with a Syrian asylum seeker, August 19, 2018)

The lucky ones who have a valid Syrian passport and want to travel to a country where a visa is required will likely face visa denials, especially by the EU and the Gulf States. The Holders of the DA visa sound like potential asylum seekers for destination countries' authorities, let alone the Syrian passport's minimal mobility. According to the Henly Passport Index, the unprivileged Syrian passport was ranked at the bottom of the 2020 ranking list along with Afghani and Iraqi ones (the Henley Passport Index 2020). One Syrian laments his frequent visa denials hyperbolically:

> "this hawk can no longer fly (referring to the Hawk of Quraish drawn on the cover of the Syrian Passport) a Syrian cannot even enter a zoo without a visa!". (personal communication with a Syrian asylum seeker, October 17, 2019)

Asylum seekers in Japan, including Syrians, have been desperately wishing to change their temporary DA visa into a more extended validity visa. They are frequently denied full-time employment, property rents, bank accounts, credit cards, and other services. Denials have caused a great sense of insecurity and haste to acquire a more privileged visa, especially since some have been renewing their annual DA visa since 2012. Marrying a Japanese national and possessing a spouse visa has been a common practice followed by all asylum seekers in Japan, too. To this end, the MOJ announced a plan to permit qualified asylum seekers to take a test and apply for the 'Specified Skilled Worker" from April 2020. (Ministry of Justice, 2020) The decision would only benefit asylum seekers with professional skills to secure a full-time job and a five-year-long visa.

Some of the informal Syrian asylum seekers have managed to obtain Long-Term Resident (LTR) visa *"Teijusha"* and reunite with their families in Japan. It is possible to change the visa status from DA to LTR after three years of possessing the DA visa. The MOJ evaluates applicants based on their income, tax payments, behavior in Japan, and convincing reasons for staying in Japan and not returning to Syria. The LTR visa is valid for five years in the case of recognized refugees, one to three years in the case of informal asylum seekers. (Watanabe, S, personal communication, March 26, 2019)

The majority of contemporary Syrians in Japan, including asylum seekers, want to stay in the country. Informal asylum seekers want to restart their lives. Married ones hope to reunite with their families. Japan's postwar reconstruction and its high level of safety both fascinate many of them as one puts it:

> "Muslim women wearing hijab could be attacked and mocked in Europe. Japan is safer for Muslim families than in Europe, and I want my children to grow up here and go to Japanese universities. They need to learn how to reconstruct Syria from Japan". (personal communication with a Syrian asylum seeker, September 16, 2018)

Recognized refugees can access higher education thanks to the UNHCR-Refugee Higher Education Program (RHEP). Thirteen Japanese universities, mostly based in the Kanto region, offer various scholarships and tuition fee waivers for a limited number of majors. UNHCR- RHEP, 2020). However, informal asylum seekers cannot access such a program or enroll in Japanese universities for financial and visa issues.

It is worth mentioning that Japan announced that it would offer a total of 150 scholarships between 2017 and 2021 for Syrian graduate students to study in Japanese universities. The announcement came on the eve of presiding the G7 Ise-Shima Summit in 2016 (Mie 2016). Through the "JISR" program, the Japan International Cooperation Agency (JICA) allocates 100 scholarships for Syrian "refugee students", those UNHCR-registered refugees in Lebanon and Jordan (JICA, 2019). The Ministry of Education (MEXT) sponsors the remaining 50 students.

Conclusion

The Japanese humanitarian response to Syria has been commendable. Also, educating Syrians in Japanese universities would highly contribute to post-conflict civil reconciliation and reconstruction. However, Tokyo's domestic asylum policy and her aid are asymmetrical. Japanese policymakers have to strike a balance between those two pillars of the international refugee regime.

The anti-refugee sentiments in Japan are attributed to the fact that the Japanese public is under-informed about mass displacement around the world. The public has no significant experience in interacting with refugees or hiring them. Thus, the opposing views on refugee resettlement in Japan should not be considered as mere xenophobia.

The successive Japanese administrations lack political will to open the doors for refugees since they prioritize sending aid to war-torn countries like Syria rather than committing to the resettlement projects. Consequently, this combination reflects itself on judicial and administrative personnel's attitude, resulting in accepting a few refugees annually and creating forms of informal asylum such as the "Syria case."

The Japanese Ministry of Justice has treated Syrians preferentially. Since they came from a full-blown conflict zone, the Ministry created an alternative policy to refugee status, namely, the "Syria case." Strict bureaucratic and judicial practices made the majority of Syrians strategically opt for the informal asylum instead of refugee status.

The informal asylum of Syrians in Japan is a case of unsupported refugee acceptance, not resettlement. Those who work, pay tax, and live without state support, are allowed to remain in Japan longer. Only hardworking Syrians can change their unprivileged temporary visas into more extended ones.

Furthermore, to deal with a severe labor shortage, the Japanese authorities permitted informal asylum seekers to stay in Japan, access the labor market, and earn money to support themselves and their families abroad. In reality, they are temporary workers.

Informal asylum seekers have achieved significant economic independence and partial self-reliance. Their lack of Japanese language ability, knowledge of domestic laws, and social support networks have hindered their integration into Japanese society. In a nutshell, the informal asylum successfully supported their livelihood but did not provide protection nor social inclusion.

Nearly 80 million people are forcibly displaced around the world. At the same time, 10 out of 60.6 million homes were either vacant or abandoned in Japan by 2019. The country will have 6.4 unfilled jobs by 2030. On the other hand, 36.1 million Japanese is 65 or older by 2020. The ratio of elderly to the total population (126 million) stands at 28.7%, the highest in the world. As the world's third-largest economy faces alarming depopulation and labor shortage, Japan needs young blood to sustain its economy. Integrated refugees would become future citizens who can contribute to the economic growth of the nation.

As an emerging migration country, Japanese academic institutions and civil society groups can play a more proactive role in asserting Japan's opportunity and burden-sharing globally. At the same time, they have little room to maneuver under the current social and political conditions.

Japan has embraced modernity while cherishing its rich cultural heritage. The country is capable of adding new values to the international refugee regime once Japanese legislators have political will. As for the Syrian case, Japan can resettle Syrian artisans and industrial workers as well as take in refugees on humanitarian grounds; this move would benefit both the host

Japanese society and preserve declining Syrian craftsmanship.[2]

Acknowledgment:

I extend my profound gratitude to many individuals who contributed to this study. Asylum seekers, NPOs/NGOs directors, lawyers and academics kindly granted me the time and tolerated my questions. I am also in debt to my supervisors at Osaka University, Prof. Akihisa Matsuno and Prof. Virgil Hawkins. Both gentlemen spared no effort to steer me in the right direction and conduct this research. My sincerest appreciation goes to Honjo International Scholarship Foundation and its kind staff for their extraordinary generosity toward me since April 2018.

References

51.3% of Japanese support bill to accept mpre foreign workers, Kyodo poll shows.(2018, November 8). *The Japan Times*.
https://www.japantimes.co.jp/news/2018/11/04/national/politics-diplomacy/51-3-japanese-support-bill-accept-foreign-workers-kyodo-poll-shows/

7.67% say Japan cannot speak with US as equals on economic issues: Mainichi survey.(2017, February 20). *The Mainichi*.
https://mainichi.jp/english/articles/20170220/p2a/00m/0na/008000c

A senior executive officer of an NPO who wished to remain anonymous, personal communication. March 24, 2019.

Abe says Japan must solve its own problems before accepting any Syria refugees. (2015. September 30). *Reuters*. https://www.reuters.com/article/us-un-assembly-japan-syria/abe-says-japan-must-solve-its-own-problems-before-accepting-any-syria-refugees-idUSKCN0RT2WK20150929

Arakaki,O. (2016). *Refugee Law and Practice in Japan*. Routledge.

Asylum Information Database (AIDA). (2019). *Country Report: Germany, 2018 Update-April 2019*. 8. Retrieved from http://www.asylumineurope.org/reports/country/germany

Asylum Information Database (AIDA). (2019). *Country Report: United Kingdom, 2018 Update-March 2019*. 9. Retrieved from
https://www.asylumineurope.org/reports/country/united-kingdom

Asylum Information Database (AIDA).(2019). *Country Report: Italy, 2018 Update-April 2019*. 79, Retrieved from http://www.asylumineurope.org/reports/country/italy

Bill to accept more foreign workers in Japan 'half-baked': opposition parties. (2018, November 1). *The Mainichi*.
https://mainichi.jp/english/articles/20181101/p2a/00m/0na/009000c

Brody,B.(2002). Opening the Door. Immigration, Ethnicity, and Globalization in Japan. Routledge. In,Beauchamp,E (Ed).

Denyer,S. Kashiwagi, A. (2018, December 8) Japan passes controversial new immigration bill to attract foreign workers. *The Washington Post*.
https://www.washingtonpost.com/world/japan-passes-controversial-new-immigration-

---

[2] For example, Aleppo Soap is an ancient industry and enjoys a good reputation among Japanese customers, mainly ladies. Mosiac arts are equally appealing to the Japanese and international consumers, too.

bill-to-attract-foreign-workers/2018/12/07/a76d8420-f9f3-11e8-863a-8972120646e0_story.html

Diplomatic Blue Book. (2020) Ministry of Foreign Affairs of Japan.

Ebuchi, T. Takeuchi, Y. Nikkei Satff Writers. (2018, October 2018). 54% of Japanese in favor of accepting more foreign workers. Nikkei Asian Review. https://asia.nikkei.com/Spotlight/Japan-immigration/54-of-Japanese-in-favor-of-accepting-more-foreign-workers2

Ford, R, personal communication, March 3, 2018.

Gibney, Matthew J. (2008). Asylum and the Expansion of Deportation in the United Kingdom. *Government and Opposition.* 43, 2, 146-167.

Hashimoto, N. (2018, May 1). *why does Japan recognise so few refugees ?.* School of Advanced Study University of London. Retrieved from https://rli.blogs.sas.ac.uk/2018/05/01/why-does-japan-recognise-so-few-refugees/

Homsi, A, personal communication. September 16, 2018.

Honma, H. (2008). Japan's Refugee Policy from Post war II to Present Day. *Forced Migration Review, No 20 Winter 2008, 23.*

Immigration Bureau, the Japanese Ministry of Justice. *Number of applicants recognized as refugees in 2017.* press release, March, 2018. P.5. Retrieved from http://www.moj.go.jp/content/001255158.pdf

Japan Association for Refugees (JAR*).*(2017, May 9). *Why Japan Refugee Recognition Rate is Low ?.* Retrieved from https://www.refugee.or.jp/jar/report/2017/06/09-0001.shtml

Japan Association for Refugees. (2018). *To Those Who Wish to Apply for Refugee Status.* Retrieved February 2018, P.26. From https://www.refugee.or.jp/for_refugees/tothose/tothose_english_1802.pdf

Japan has highest ratio of elderly people. (2020, September 20). *NHK.* https://www3.nhk.or.jp/nhkworld/en/news/20200920_20/

Japan International Cooperation Agency (JICA). Japanese Initiative for the future of Syrian Refugees (JISR). December 15, 2019, Retrieved from https://www.jica.go.jp/syria/english/office/others/jisr.html

Japan Lawyers Network for Refugees. (2020). *Statistics Section.* Japan Lawyer Network for Refugees. http://www.jlnr.jp/stat/

JAR. (2017, September 10). *Why Japan recognizes only a few refugees? Institutional challenges.* Retrieved from https://www.refugee.or.jp/jar/report/2017/09/10-0000.shtml

Kamata,T. (2018, November 20). What's at stake: inside Shinzo Abe's efforts to bring more foreign workers into Japan. *NHK World-Japan.* https://www3.nhk.or.jp/nhkworld/en/news/backstories/302/

Lloyd, G. (2020, May 19). Shizuoka town determined to put empty houses to good use. *Japan Today.* https://japantoday.com/category/features/lifestyle/shizuoka-town-determined-to-put-empty-houses-to-good-use

M, Ishikawa, personal communication, March 27, 2019.

Mie, A.(2016, May 20). Japan to take in 150 Syrians as exchange students after criticism of harsh refugee policy. *The Japan Times.* https://www.japantimes.co.jp/news/2016/05/20/national/japan-take-150-syrians-exchange-students-criticism-harsh-refugee-policy/#.Xg1-RvxS_iU

Ministry of Justice.(2020). *[Important Notice] Qualifications of Candidacy for Examination will be Expanded from April 1, 2020.* Retrieved from http://www.moj.go.jp/nyuukokukanri/kouhou/nyuukokukanri01_00135.html

Motrita, T.(2003). Iranian Immigrant Workers in Japan and Their Networks.Goodman,R & Peach,C& Tanaka,A& White, P. *Global Japan.* 159-160. Routledge.

Mukae,R. (2001). *Japan Refugee Policy: To be of the World.* European Press Academic Publishing.

Osumi, M. (2019, March 29). Probe reveals 759 cases of suspected abuse and 171 deaths of foreign trainees in Japan. *The Japan Times.*

https://www.japantimes.co.jp/news/2019/03/29/national/probe-reveals-759-cases-suspected-abuse-foreign-trainees-japan-171-deaths/

Personal communication with a Syrian asylum seeker, August 19, 2018.

Personal communication with a Syrian asylum seeker, June 2, 2020.

Personal communication with a Syrian asylum seeker, May 12, 2018.

Refugee Assistance Headquarters. (2020, July 17) *Assistance for Applicants for Recognition of Refugee Status.*Retrieved from https://www.rhq.gr.jp/assistance-for-applicants-for-recognition-of-refugee-status/

Personal communication with a Syrian asylum seeker, November 9, 2019.

Personal communication with a Syrian asylum seeker, October 17, 2019.

Personal communication with a Syrian asylum seeker, September 16, 2018.

Personal communication with a Syrian family, January 2019.

Personal communication with two asylum seekers, July 2018

Retrieved from Court Rejection verdict of a Syrian asylum seeker. February 2020.

Sellek,Y.(2001). *Migrant Labour in Japan.* Palgrave Macmillan.

Shogo W, personal communication, April 25, 2019.

Statistics of Japan (Japanese Government Statistics). (2019, December). *Statistics of Foreigners Residents in Japan.* 19-12-01-2. 19-12-02-2. 19-12-04. Retrieved from https://www.e-stat.go.jp/stat-search/files?page=1&layout=datalist&toukei=00250012&tstat=000001018034&cycle=1&year=20190&month=24101212&tclass1=000001060399

Sugiyama, S. (2018, December 31). Japan's denial of immigration reality echoes Germany's experience with 'guest workers'. *The Japan Times.* https://www.japantimes.co.jp/news/2018/12/31/national/japans-denial-immigration-reality-echoes-germanys-experience-guest-workers/

Takeda, I. (1989). Japan's Response to Refugees and Political Asylum Seekers. In Weiner .M (Ed) and Hanami, T (Ed). *Temporary Workers of Future Citizens.* 436. New York University Press.

Takeda,I. (1989). Japan's Response to Refugees and Political Asylum Seekers. In Weiner .M (Ed) and Hanami,T (Ed). *Temporary Workers of Future Citizens.* 436. New York University Press.

Takegaki, H, personal communication, March 25, 2019.

Takizawa, S. (2018). Japan's Refugee Policy: Issues and Outlook. Japan's Contributions to International Peace and Security Series.7. http://www2.jiia.or.jp/en/pdf/digital_library/peace/Saburo_Takizawa-Japan_s_Refugee_Policy_Issues_and_Outlook.pdf

Tanaka, C.(2018, March 20). Syrian asylum-seekers' bid for refugee status rejected by Tokyo court.*The Japan Times.* https://www.japantimes.co.jp/news/2018/03/20/national/crime-legal/syrian-asylum-seekers-bid-refugee-status-rejected-tokyo-court/#.XcpqDtVS_iU

The Embassy of Japan in the Syrian Arab Republic. (2012). *Bilateral Relations.* Retrieved from https://www.sy.emb-japan.go.jp/summary.htm

The European Commission. (2018, August 8). *EMN Ad-Hoc Query on The decision-making practice on Syrians avoiding military service as conscientious objectors.* Retrieved from https://ec.europa.eu/home-affairs/sites/homeaffairs/files/2018.1327_-_the_decision-making_practice_on_syrians_avoiding_military_service_as_conscientious_objectors.pdf

The Henley Passport Index. (2020). Global Ranking 2020. The Henley Passport Index. https://www.henleypassportindex.com/passport

難民認定制度の運用の更なる見直し後の状況について

The Japanese Ministry of Justice. *The Situation after Revisions of the Refugee Recognition System.* Retrieved August 8, 2018, P.3. http://www.moj.go.jp/nyuukokukanri/kouhou/nyuukokukanri03_00116.html

UNHCR.(2005, August 2005)Handbook for Self-reliance.

UNHCR.(2019).*Global Trends: Forced Diplacement in 2018*. Retrieved from
    https://www.unhcr.org/globaltrends2018/
UNHCR-Refugee Higher Education Program. October 9, 2019. Retrieved from
    http://rhep-japanforunhcr.org/en/
USA for UNHCR. (2020). *Syria Refugee Crisis*. USA for UNHCR the UN Refugee Agency.
    https://www.unrefugees.org/emergencies/syria/
Watanabe, S, personal communication, March 26, 2019.
Yamaguchi,K, personal communication, March 29, 2019
(データを読む　世論調査から）難民の受け入れ　変わらない消極姿勢
(Reading public opinion polls) Negative Stand about Refugee Acceptance has not changed
    Asahi Newspaper. (2016, Januray 30). *The Asahi Shimbun.*
    https://www.asahi.com/articles/DA3S12184937.html

CHAPTER 4

MAKING DIASPORA POLICIES WITHOUT KNOWING THE DIASPORA? THE CASE OF SRI LANKA

Pavithra Jayawardena

Introduction

Sri Lanka is a country with over one million diaspora living permanently outside, mostly in Europe, North America and Australasia (Reeves, 2013). The number of the diaspora constitutes a 20:1 Sri Lankan total population to Sri Lankan diaspora ratio, the highest such in South Asia (Reeves, 2013). Despite this significant population to diaspora ratio, Sri Lanka does not have well-developed diaspora policies to reach its diaspora members. The dual citizenship policy stands as the only diaspora outreach policy of Sri Lanka. Sri Lanka introduced the dual citizenship policy in 1987 (Government of Sri Lanka, 1987b). It enabled Sri Lankan emigrants who have decided to naturalize in another country to resume or retain their Sri Lankan citizenship. As discussed in this chapter, the government's motivation to grant dual citizenship is instrumental. The chapter proposes one reason for this matter, as the Sri Lankan government attempt to cater to emigrants' expectations, assuming that emigrants have more instrumental desires for dual citizenship. For example, the state-level initiatives show that the government assumes emigrants who wish to obtain Sri Lankan dual citizenship do so because they have to buy and/or keep land/property, invest or initiate businesses in Sri Lanka.

However, no academic or policy level research has been conducted so far to study the reasons Sri Lankan diaspora members obtain dual citizenship. With no scientific knowledge about Sri Lankan diaspora members' expectations for and interests in dual citizenship, the government's instrumental assumption stated above cannot be justified. Consequently, this lack of knowledge hinders evaluating Sri Lankan dual citizenship policy's effectiveness. Hence, this research attempts to study Sri Lankan diaspora members' perceptions about the Sri Lankan dual citizenship to measure the policy's effectiveness. The data for this qualitative research were collected and analysed using the constructivist grounded theory (Silverman, 2011). The findings of the study suggest that Sri Lankan diaspora members' perceptions about the dual citizenship are different from the Sri Lankan government's instrumental assumptions of diaspora members' interests. Participants revealed that they have more non-instrumental reasons (e.g. sense of belonging) to obtain Sri Lankan dual citizenship while the government has more instrumental assumptions (e.g. investing).

The chapter beings with a description of research methods used to collect and analyse data in this study. Secondly, it gives an overview of Sri Lankan emigration with a specific discussion about the Sri Lankan dual citizenship policy. Thirdly, I present the findings of the study; participants' interests towards the Sri Lankan dual citizenship policy, followed by the conclusion.

Methodology

This research primarily employs a qualitative research design to understand Sri Lankan emigrants' complex and multi-layered views about Sri Lankan dual citizenship. Qualitative studies are aimed at understanding the "complex world of human experience and behaviour from … those who are involved in the situation of interest" (Krauss, 2005, p.764). Qualitative studies are empirical in general because they exist in natural settings (Toma, 2006). They, therefore, help us understand "individual diversity and the nuance of social context" (Stein & Mankowski, 2004, p.21).

I use a constructivist grounded theory approach in collecting, analysing and interpreting data. This approach suggests viewing data as constructed. It acknowledges the notion of multiple realities, and it emphasizes the reflexivity. According to this approach, data is not simply out there in the world, waiting to be discovered (Silverman, 2011). Hence it suggests that conducting research (data itself, data collection and data interpretation) flows from views and values and therefore not neutral in any means. Therefore, in analysing data, constructivism suggests that the researcher should locate him/herself within the inquiry without locating him/herself as an outsider (Silverman, 2011). Constructivist theorists do not believe that a researcher can remain neutral observers and look at data/inquiry as outsiders. Also, the approach suggests, by locating themselves inside the investigation, qualitative researchers can get much closer to the data and the studied phenomenon. Consequently, constructivist researchers can get an in-depth understanding of the participants' meanings and actions.

This research used interviews as the primary method to collect data from Sri Lankan emigrants. Interviewing is the central resource of comprehending knowledge in social sciences (Atkinson & Silverman, 1997). It is considered the primary method that researchers use to collect rich and in-depth experiential data (Fontana & Frey, 2005). According to Rapley (2011), interviews are social encounters where respondents share their accounts or versions of the past, present, and future actions, experiences, feelings and thoughts. Interviews are an essential research method to receive information which researchers would not otherwise know; to reach the knowledge in people's heads, and to hear about their experiences, feelings, and beliefs that guide their behaviours (Holý & Stuchlik, 1983).

The data were collected through semi-structured interviews with fifty-one Sri Lankan emigrants residing in Australia and New Zealand. Fifty-one interviews were conducted because the scholars recommend a sample of thirty to sixty to collect rich data through semi-structured interviews (Guest, Bunce, & Johnson, 2006; Morse, 2000). Also, I recruited participants from only first-generation. This is to avoid different generational dynamics over-complicating this study. As migration scholars have found, migrants from different generations have different meanings and actions as they have received different migratory experiences (Bartley & Spoonley, 2008; Portes & Zhou, 1993).

Interviews were conducted in Melbourne and Sydney in Australia and Auckland and Wellington in New Zealand. These cities were selected because of the high population of Sri Lankan migrants living there. In Australia, Victoria has the highest number of Sri Lankan immigrants: 43,991 Sri Lankans (51% of the total Sri Lankan immigrant population in Australia). Victoria is followed by New South Wales, with nearly 23,704 Sri Lankan immigrants (Australian Government, 2014). Auckland is the most popular city among Sri Lankans in New Zealand, with 61.2% (6,903 people) of the total Sri Lankan immigrant population (Statistics New Zealand, 2013). Wellington is the second most popular city as it hosts 16.8% (1,893 people) of New Zealand's Sri Lankan immigrant population (Statistics New Zealand, 2013).

The sample was recruited through purposive sampling to ensure the data can reflect the diversity of the Sri Lankan diaspora community. 60% of the participants were ethnically Sinhalese, and 40% were Tamil participants. While all the participants were first-generation emigrants, I recruited emigrants who have arrived in their host country (Australia or New Zealand) in different years from the 1960s to 2017. To get a rich data set, I recruited emigrants who are of different citizenship statuses such as migrants who have become dual citizens, citizens of the host country only, who decided to remain as permanent residents in the host country or who arrived in as refugees etc.

Snow-balling technique was used to expand the connections with the members of the Sri Lankan immigrant community. To prevent the common weakness of the snow-balling (ending up with likeminded participants), I used different entry points to enter the Sri Lankan community. On the one hand, I used my personal contacts to find more members. On the other hand, I connected with different types of Sri Lankan migrant organizations in the four cities and found members through those organizations. I also found more members through connecting with the Sri Lankan officials in the host countries. In analysing the data, I used thematic analysis. According to Roulston (2010), thematic analysis is perhaps one of the most commonly used approaches to analyse data qualitatively. Themes can be generated in multiple ways. Through sorting data into codes, categories and themes, this approach helps to reorganize the data into a thematic representation of findings (Roulston, 2010).

Sri Lankan emigration and dual citizenship policy

Sri Lanka has a population of 20.7 million (United Nations Development Programme, 2016). It is a multi-cultural, multi-ethnic and a multi-religious country with 74.9% Sinhalese (majority ethnic group), 11.2% Tamils, 4.1% Indian Tamils, 9.3% Moor and 0.5% others (Department of Census and Statistics, 2012). All these ethnic groups have produced migrants over the last few decades. The total number of Sri Lankan emigrants is uncertain. According to Reeves (2013), there are three million Sri Lankan emigrants. However, this number includes the two million temporary labour migrants working in the Gulf area. This chapter does not pay attention to the temporary labour Sri Lankan emigrants. It also looks at diaspora members who have already permanently settled outside Sri Lanka or wish to do so. According to the International Crisis Group (2010), two million Sri Lankan diaspora members are permanently settled outside Sri Lanka. According to Reeves (2013), the total number is one million, and they live scattered across the Americas (500,000), Europe (400,000) and Australasia (70,000). Sri Lankan migrants produce a remarkable diaspora population given that today approximately one in every twenty Sri Lankans permanently resides abroad (Reeves, 2013; Sriskandarajah, 2002).

Sri Lankan diaspora is a diverse community. To understand the diversity of the Sri Lankan diaspora, it is important to understand the history of Sri Lankan emigration. Five waves can be seen in Sri Lankan emigration (Wanasinghe-Pasqual & Jayawardena, 2017). The first wave occurred after Sri Lanka received independence from British colonisers in 1948. It was mainly consisted of Sri Lankan Burgher ethnic people who emigrated to Western countries such as Britain and Australia. They emigrated with the fear that they will be discriminated by the majority ethnic group/s in Sri Lanka with the power transfer from colonial masters to local people (Gamage, 2002; Pinnawala, 1984). The second wave of migration occurred after 1956 when the Sri Lankan government introduced controversial national language reforms (Sinhala Only Act) that made the majority's language (Sinhalese) the national language (Wayland, 2004). People who were not comfortable in using Sinhalese language decided to emigrate. The third wave occurred in the early 1970s. During this time, the government intervened in all the industries and introduced drastic nationalization reforms (Athukorala, Prema-chandra Jayasuriya, 2000). Due to the political and economic insecurities, professionals both Sinhalese and Tamils who were not confident about the future of the country decided to emigrate (Gamage, 1998). Western democratic countries such as Great Britain, Australia, Canada, Switzerland and Germany were their prime choices (Henayaka-Lochbihler & Lambusta, 2004).

The fourth wave that occurred during the 1980s marked the zenith of the Sri Lankan emigration. During the 1980s, two armed conflicts erupted: one in the northern part of the country (which later turned into civil war) and the other in the southern part of Sri Lanka (Siriwardhana & Wickramage, 2014; Sriskandarajah, 2002). These two conflicts added a new layer of emigrants to the Sri Lankan migration history, the forced migrants. The northern conflict led many Tamils to migrate on humanitarian grounds, as refugees or asylum seekers while the southern conflict led some Sinhalese to migrate for similar security reasons (Gamage, 1998; Sriskandarajah, 2002). Meanwhile, the previous professional emigrant category (created in second and third waves) also continued the outflow (Gamage, 1998). However, unlike the previous waves, Tamils' migration significantly surpassed Sinhalese migration in 1980s. Sriskandarajah (2002) notes that Tamil migration from Sri Lanka specifically after 1983, does not only contain those who have sought asylum on arrival in the West through informal routes but also skilled migrants who arrived on family reunion programs and as political refugees. Another main difference, as opposed to the previous waves, was that the emigrants in the fourth wave had a united ethnic identity either as a Sinhalese or a Tamil due to their domestic experience at the time (Wayland, 2004). While all the above-stated migrant categories continued the outflow, the fifth wave occurred in the early 2000s. This wave includes a considerable proportion of young Sri Lankans who started emigrating due to the dissatisfaction of the domestic conditions (Pingama, 2016). Also, a trend of illegal migration (e.g. to Australia by boat) emerged and this continues until today (Howie, 2013).

As explained above, Sri Lankan migration waves have been caused by a multitude of economic, political, social, and security push factors. However, ethnic conflict constitutes the primary reason for Tamils' emigration (Sriskandarajah, 2002). Ethnic tensions continued to be evident between Sinhalese and Tamil immigrants in host countries (Orjuela, 2008). Therefore Reeves (2013) notes that Sri Lankan diaspora does not function as a single entity; instead it functions separately as the Sinhalese diaspora and the Sri Lankan Tamil diaspora. Consequently, Sri Lankan emigrants from separate ethnic groups tend to network only with the relevant ethnic community in the host countries (Reeves, 2013).

Sri Lanka does not have a variety of developed diaspora outreach policies. However, the country offers dual citizenship for its diaspora members who wish to continue their Sri Lankan citizenship. Dual citizenship was introduced in 1987 (Government of Sri Lanka, 1987b). By the year 1987, Sri Lankan emigrants showed a huge interest in continuing to be a Sri Lankan citizen. Until 1987, if an emigrant who is permanently living in another country obtains citizenship of that country, Sri Lankan citizenship was automatically cancelled. There was no alternative way to remain as a Sir Lankan citizen, no matter how seriously an emigrant wanted to.

Then Prime Minister R. Premadasa declared in the parliament as follows:

"there are a large number of Sri Lankans who have obtained citizenship in other countries but still regret that they do not have citizenship in their own motherland ... such people [emigrants who have become citizens in other countries] would like to invest in various projects in this country and contribute to the wellbeing of the country. The purpose is to get their participation. Such people will be an asset to this country. And we thought that this request made to us by our own citizens should be entertained" (Government of Sri Lanka, 1987a)

In his speech in justifying the introduction of dual citizenship for Sri Lankan emigrants, Prime Minister used terms such as *motherland* and *our own citizens* in an emotive form. Conversely, the execution of the dual citizenship, as discussed following, does not show any sign of recognizing Sri Lankan emigrants' emotive desires to obtain dual citizenship.

With the introduction of the dual citizenship, Minister of Internal Affairs was granted the power to offer dual citizenship for the interested emigrants. Emigrants who want to become Sri Lankan dual citizens had to apply for dual citizenship. They were enabled to either retain or resume the Sri Lankan dual citizenship (Government of Sri Lanka, 1987b). If the emigrant was in the process of becoming a citizen of another country, but have not yet become, he/she could apply to retain the Sri Lankan citizenship (Government of Sri Lanka, 1987b). If the emigrant had already become a citizen of another country and as a result of that, their Sri Lankan citizenship has been ceased, they can request to resume the Sri Lankan citizenship (Government of Sri Lanka, 1987b). The Minister of Internal Affairs had to handle case by case depending on the merits of each case. According to the citizenship (amendment) act (1987), "...the Minister may make the declaration for which the application is made if he is satisfied that the making of such declaration would, in all the circumstances of the case, be of benefit to Sri Lanka."

I argue that the government's interpretation of the phrase *be of benefit to Sri Lanka* is more instrumental. A piece of evidence is the Sri Lankan dual citizenship application (Department of Immigration and Emigration Sri Lanka, 2018). The application manifests that the government's expectations to benefit from their emigrants' instrumental interest in becoming a Sri Lankan dual citizen. The dual citizenship application has seven eligibility categories through which Sri Lankan emigrants can request dual citizenship.

None of those categories intends to assess or recognize emigrants' non-instrumental interests.

The seven categories are as follows:

1. exceeds the age of 55

2. fulfils the academic/professional qualifications (minimum one-year diploma or higher or any professional qualification)

3. owns assets/immovable properties in Sri Lanka worth Rs. 2.5 million or above

4. has a fixed deposit of Rs. 2.5 million or above for a minimum of 03 year period in any of the commercial banks approved by the central bank of Sri Lanka

5. has a fixed deposit of USD 25,000 or above for a minimum of 03 year period under Non Resident Foreign Currency (NRFC), Resident Foreign Currency Account (RFC) or Senior Foreign Invest Deposit Account (SFIDA) in any of the commercial banks approved by the central bank of Sri Lanka.

6. has invested USD 25,000 or above for a minimum of 03-year period under TB (Treasury bonds) or SIA (Security Investment Account)

7. qualifying by way of the spouse of the applicant or as an unmarried child under the age of 22 of the applicant

Out of these seven categories, two categories (No. 1 and 7) are accordingly for older people and for the spouses and children of the successful applicants. All the other five categories (No. 2,3,4,5 and 6) require professional, academic, property or financial evidence for a candidate to be eligible to apply for Sri Lankan dual citizenship. This means the Minister of Internal Affairs will assess those who have professional or academic certificates and/or pieces of evidence of property ownership, fixed deposits or investments as eligible dual citizens who are of benefit to Sri Lanka.

Under this categorization, emigrants without academic, professional qualifications or property, fixed deposits or investments, not exceed the age of 55 or a spouse of a child of a successful applicant, have no pathway to becoming Sri Lankan dual citizens. The current categorization does not take into account emigrants' non-instrumental reasons such as emotive interest to become a Sri Lankan dual citizenship or their sense of belonging. A successful applicant should also pay nearly 2000 USD - a high price as a fee to obtain dual citizenship (Department of Immigration and Emigration Sri Lanka, 2018). It is not clearly justified as to why the government gives priority to emigrants who have instrumental evidence and financial capability when offering dual citizenship. Therefore, I argue that the government expects for Sri Lanka to benefit from emigrants who have instrumental potentials such as property or investments. This suggests that the government of Sri Lanka considers *be of benefit to Sri Lanka* in its instrumental sense.

Another evidence is the way Sri Lankan government temporarily discontinued granting dual citizenship in 2011 (Ganeshathasan & Welikala, 2017; Rajasingham, 2013). Officially declared reason for this shut down was the government's realization that dual citizens no longer serve its purpose (David, 2011). The main argument was that dual citizens return to Sri Lanka only to buy properties and they avoid higher taxes (David, 2011), and therefore dual citizenship does not bring any 'benefit to Sri Lanka' anymore (Ganeshathasan & Welikala, 2017). This again verified that the phrase 'be of benefit to Sri Lanka' has an instrumental meaning mostly.

The temporarily discontinued dual citizenship issuing was reopened in 2015 with a new law. Sri Lankan dual citizens now cannot be elected as a member of parliament or to sit and vote in the parliament (Government of Sri Lanka, 2015). I argue that the reason for this decision was once again instrumental. It was suggested that Sri Lankan politicians with dual citizenship in another country could steal public money in Sri Lanka and flee the country when necessary as they can find protection there (Jayanath, 2015).

This evidence suggests that the government of Sri Lanka expects its dual citizenship policy to bring instrumental benefits to Sri Lanka. This could be because the government seems to assume that emigrants who wish to obtain Sri Lankan dual citizenship predominantly have instrumental interests to do so. On the other hand, there is no evidence in the dual citizenship policy to show that the government is considering the emigrants' non-instrumental interests such as the sense of belonging or loyalty in offering them the dual citizenship.

Findings and discussion: Sri Lankan emigrants' views about dual citizenship

Participants of this research show that their main interests to obtain Sri Lankan dual citizenship are different from the government's interests. As explained earlier, the Sri Lankan government expects emigrants to be interested in dual citizenship for instrumental reasons such as buying property, investing or doing businesses in Sri Lanka. However, most of the participants of this research revealed that they have more non-instrumental interests than instrumental interests. Below, I first explain the varied non-instrumental reasons, as mentioned by the participants. Then, I explain the limited instrumental reasons mentioned by some of the participants.

Non-instrumental interests

Forty-six of the fifty-one participants noted the sense of belonging as the key reason that encourages them to retain or resume Sri Lankan dual citizenship. Three aspects influenced participants' sense of belonging towards Sri Lanka: the sense of belonging towards (i) *the people* (ii) *the land* and (iii) *the culture*. It should be noted that these three components of the sense of belonging are highly over-lapping. For example, a participant's sense of belonging to *the land* can be a result of his/her relationships with *the people* or his/her preference for *the culture*. Even though there can be such overlaps and subtle relationships between the three components, this categorization (*people, land* and *culture*) only attempts to explore different non-instrumental aspects of Sri Lankan emigrants' sense of belonging towards their Sri Lankan dual citizenship.

Sense of belonging to the people

Many participants wanted to become a Sri Lankan dual citizen to ensure their legal right to travel to Sri Lanka at any given time. For these participants, travelling to Sri Lanka was essential to continue their sense of belonging to the people in Sri Lanka. People here are two folded: (i) those who participants have direct contact with, such as family, friends, relatives, neighbours and (ii) those who participants do not have direct connections with, such as the other co-members of the Sri Lankan society. Jenkins (2004) provides a useful explanation to understand the differences of a person's belonging to the people who he/she knows and does not know personally. According to him, in everyday life, a person's belonging to the people he/she knows personally, begins with a personalized experience; in which case, they identify each other as fellow individuals than any reference to their collective identification. Vice versa, in identifying others with whom they have no direct connection, people tend to first view them as members of their collectivity, as contemporaries. The findings of this study strongly support Jenkins's analysis. Following, I first explain my participants' belonging to the people they knew personally and secondly, I explain their belonging to their fellow citizens in the Sri Lankan society.

As mentioned above, one of the frequently shared reasons for participants to remain as Sri Lankan dual citizens is the keen interest to continue their ties with people they have direct contacts with. This includes their family, friends, relatives and neighbours. Participants wanted to maintain relationships with these people because they had a strong sense of belonging towards them. The most recurrent tie was the relationship with the participants' immediate family. Except for a few participants, others had their parents and siblings living in Sri Lanka. Priyadarshani (40), a female Sinhalese New Zealand permanent resident said she would become a New Zealand citizen only if she can also obtain the Sri Lankan dual citizenship. The main reason for her to continue the Sri Lankan citizenship, as she said was "... my parents are living [in Sri Lanka, so] I have commitments [there.]" Priyadarshani thought that having Sri Lankan dual citizenship would allow her to visit Sri Lanka at any time. It will also enable her to stay there as long as she wants. Some other participants mentioned they wish to continue relationship not only with their immediate family but also with their relatives, neighbours and friends. To continue such relationships, participants thought visiting Sri Lanka frequently is a must. Thus, they considered the legal right Sri Lankan dual citizenship provides for them to travelling back and forth to Sri Lanka to be essential.

Many Tamil participants also showed that their need to obtain dual citizenship is based on their relationships with the people in Sri Lanka. Shiva (60), a male Tamil New Zealand citizen, said "from my young age, all my friends and family friends ... my family, my wife's parents, brothers ... relations, friends are there [in Sri Lanka] and I have to go to the place where I was born."

However, it is essential to note that participants who are not Sri Lankan citizens but who are Australian or New Zealand citizens, can quickly get an on-arrival visitor visa to enter and stay up to 30 days (Department of Immigration and Emigration Sri Lanka, 2019). Nonetheless, many participants mentioned that they want to make sure they can stay in Sri Lanka for more than 30 days without any visa restriction. For example, Pathum, a male Sinhalese immigrant who has requested refugee status in New Zealand said "if I go to Sri Lanka ... 30 days will not be enough because I have a lot of relatives there. I need a lot of time there." Some other participants shared this concern with Pathum. Therefore, they expressed that having Sri Lankan dual citizenship would let them stay in Sri Lanka for more than 30 days without any issue.

Dinesh, a male Sinhalese New Zealand citizen, also wished to obtain dual citizenship because he had his relatives to visit in Sri Lanka. He still has not been able to get dual citizenship, mainly for two reasons. Firstly, as Dinesh revealed, he does not have a category to apply for dual citizenship. Dinesh has come to New Zealand as a skilled migrant with years of experience as a pastry chef. Apart from his skill, he neither has paper documents for his professional qualifications nor fixed deposits, property or investments in Sri Lanka. Thus, under the current categorization of the dual citizenship application, he does not have a category to become a Sri Lankan dual citizen. Secondly, even if he applied and his request was approved, Dinesh said he does not have enough money to obtain it at this time. He said, to get the dual citizenship for his entire family (Dinesh, his wife and three children) he needs at least around 3000 USD. For Dinesh, its "not affordable" now but he expects to "apply in the future."

Some participants mentioned that their sense of belonging is not only limited to the people they know but to the people they do not know personally. For example, Darshi's sense of belonging was not only a result of her close ties with the people she has direct contacts with. She, a female Sinhalese New Zealand and a Sri Lankan citizen revealed to have a strong feeling of the sense of belonging to the other Sri Lankan citizens in the home society. She believes that she shares so many commonalities with the other co-members of the home society. Darshi said:

"If [I] walk in the street in Sri Lanka, [I] have the feeling that [I] know them, although [I] don't know them personally. [I] know that they are someone among us ... Sri Lankans... I don't know, there is no strange feeling in Sri Lanka because that is our country."

Darshi shows a keen interest to continue her relationship with the co-members of the Sri Lankan society with whom she shares a common culture and a history. As a result, she has obtained the Sri Lankan dual citizenship. It can also be argued that the desire to continue the relations with the co-members is a product of participants' interest to continue their home country identity.

Praveena, a female Sinhalese New Zealand resident shared something similar. Praveena said, in Sri Lanka, unlike New Zealand, she gets the feeling of living among the people she knows. Praveena said "[in Sri Lanka] there are people, you can hear them, you can feel them." Praveena did not talk about the people she knows personally but about the other co-members in her home society. She thinks she shares many cultural similarities with them. For Praveena, becoming a Sri Lankan dual citizen is a way to continue her sense of belonging to the people she shares many commonalities with.

However, while Darshi and Praveena talked positively about their sense of belonging to the co-members of the Sri Lankan society, some participants shared an opposing view. Specifically, some Tamil participants explained how traumatic experiences with co-members had affected their perceptions negatively. Many Tamil participants revealed that they have negative views about the Sinhalese people as co-members of their home society. These negative perceptions were based on their experiences and thoughts about ethnic discrimination and majority-minority problems in Sri Lanka. Many Tamil participants viewed Sinhalese people as "racist," "ethno-nationalistic" and "undemocratic." For example, Shivakumar, a male Tamil Australian citizen, thinks Sinhalese people to be "racist, very aggressive and unable to stand other opinions." According to Shivakumar "[now the rivalry] is not only between Tamils and Sinhalese [but] even between Sinhalese [themselves]. If there are two different [ideological] groups, they [Sinhalese] kill each other. They just do not think twice [about it]." Shivakumar thinks

Sinhalese people are not democratic. He thinks, many Sinhalese people do not respect other's opinions. For this reason, Shivakumar does not exhibit a sense of belonging to the co-members of the home society. Consequently, he does not want to be a Sri Lankan dual citizen.

Saranya shared a similar thought to Shivakumar's. Saranya is a female, Tamil New Zealand citizen who claimed refugee status in New Zealand. She first expressed her negative view about Sinhalese people for "accusing Tamils, Tamils, Tamils" of everything unnecessarily. Then similar to Shivakumar, Saranya said, not only Sinhalese people can tolerate their minority Tamil people, many Sinhalese people cannot even tolerate opposing views of other Sinhalese people. She said "now see what is happening. Their own thing, they [Sinhalese] are fighting. Who is suffering?" She meant how Sinhalese politicians from different parties fight against each other because of their greed for power. As a result of these negative perceptions, Saranya does not want to obtain Sri Lankan dual citizenship, as she does not think she wants to continue her relationship with co-members in the Sri Lankan society.

The above examples show that the majority of Sinhalese participants' sense of belonging about being a Sri Lankan citizen is due to their positive relationships with the people. For many of them, it is mainly due to their ties with their family, friends, relatives and neighbours. For some, it is also due to their sense of belonging to the other co-members of the home society. In comparison to the Sinhalese participants, Tamil participants did not have positive belonging feelings about their fellow co-members of the society (specifically with Sinhalese) but their immediate family and friends.

Sense of belonging to the land

The second recurrent non-instrumental reason that encouraged participants to become Sri Lankan dual citizens was their belonging to the homeland. In terms of belonging to the land, both Sinhalese and Tamil participants shared similar views. The term motherland was often used by participants to refer to Sri Lanka. For many, it is because the land was associated in many ways with their birth and childhood. For others, there were specific geographic locations of Sri Lanka such as religious places and heritage sites that mark their unique bond with Sri Lanka.

Participants who used the term motherland did so with a robust patriotic meaning. Not only Sinhalese participants but also many Tamil participants, even refugees who have had discriminatory experiences in Sri Lanka, used the term motherland to refer to Sri Lanka. Saranya, is a female, Tamil New Zealand citizen who arrived in New Zealand as a refugee. She decided to flee Sri Lanka with her two children because of the civil war. She expressed her strong dislike towards the majority Sinhalese people, including the Sri Lankan government, for not securing Tamil citizens' minority rights. Even though Saranya had a negative perception about the Sinhalese people, simultaneously, she also had a strong positive impression about the land of Sri Lanka. She referred to Sri Lanka as her "motherland." She said "it is our motherland. you can't forget your mother, mother language, people, everything." Her interest in obtaining Sri Lankan dual citizenship is to continue this special relationship with the motherland.

The use of the term motherland to refer to one's home country is an expression of an intense patriotism towards the home country. One does not have many mothers, but only one. Also, mothers are not replaceable. Especially in South Asian culture, the mother is the symbol of respect. Children are always obliged to respect their mother. Saranya's opposing views about the people (negative perceptions) and the land (positive perceptions) also show the complexity of her relationship with home citizenship. She has been able to continue her patriotic attachment to the land of the home country while simultaneously continuing to dislike a group of co-members (the Sinhalese people) in the same society. This also challenges the general Sri Lankan majority public opinion against Sri Lankan refugees who are living outside the country. According to this opinion, refugees who left Sri Lanka (specifically Tamil refugees) do not love Sri Lanka. As a result, they often attempt to damage the identity of Sri Lanka. However, Saranya's example shows that refugees' attachments with the home country are more complex.

Amal (33), a male Sinhalese based in Melbourne also used the term motherland to refer to Sri Lanka. He wants to obtain Sri Lankan dual citizenship because "… [He does not] want to die in this country [Australia]. [He] wants to die in [his] motherland [Sri Lanka]." Conversely, Amal also expressed his keen interest to become an Australian citizen. Understanding Amal's interest in becoming an Australian citizen is helpful to understand his patriotic views towards home citizenship. For Amal, the main objective of Australian citizenship acquisition is to let his only child enjoy the benefits (specifically education) of being an Australian citizen – an instrumental reason. Amal thinks the education system in Sri Lanka needs to be developed. In comparison to Sri Lanka's education system, he believes the Australian system is more advanced and globally recognized. However, Amal's negative instrumental views about the education system in Sri Lanka has not curtailed his sense of belonging to his homeland. Even though he expects to obtain Australian citizenship for the sake of his son's education, Amal said he always wants to go back to Sri Lanka. The wish to die in his motherland as a home country citizen is an example of his loyalty and belonging to his home country.

Both Saranya and Amal used the term motherland to express their strong patriotism to Sri Lanka. While many other participants also used the term motherland with a similar patriotic meaning, Saranya's and Amal's views were unique because of the contrasting views they held. For example, they held both negative perceptions about the instrumental prospects such as violation of equal rights of citizens, lower standards of education they received as Sri Lankan citizens as well as positive perceptions about non-instrumental prospects such as love and belonging to the homeland. Irrespective of their negative opinions about instrumental opportunities, both Saranya and Amal wish to obtain Sri Lankan dual citizenship. This suggests, in making their decision of retaining or resuming their Sri Lankan citizenship, their non-instrumental interest (belonging to the land) has taken presidency over their instrumental interests.

For some other participants, obtaining Sri Lankan dual citizenship was a means of continuing their bond with where they were born and grew up. Participants revealed they have a strong and emotional attachment for the land of Sri Lanka because it was where they were born and grew up. Many Sinhalese and Tamils, both male and female, whether they arrived in the host country a few decades ago or relatively recently, as skilled migrants or refugees repeatedly mentioned that their attachment to Sri Lanka comes from their childhood memories of the land. They showed their keen interest to endure that non-instrumental relationship as long as they can.

The main reason for Udari, a female Sinhalese Australian citizen, to obtain the Sri Lankan dual citizenship, as she says is because "that is where we were born. That's our motherland. We do not want to lose the connection…" Darshi, a female Sinhalese Australian and Sri Lankan citizen also said, Sri Lanka is "everything" to her, because "… that is our country. That's where we grew up…" Anupa, a male Sinhalese New Zealand permanent resident, said "it's the place (Sri Lanka) you grew up, that's yours… Sri Lanka has given me a lot… a way of life, the culture, and that's what I am and who I am…" His views about Sri Lanka was full of patriotic spirit. Comparing home and host citizenship, Anupa mentioned that he needs to become a New Zealand citizen for instrumental reasons only. He thought obtaining the New Zealand passport will be beneficial for his children in the future. Despite to it, he said, "a bigger part of [him to] still [be] there [in Sri Lanka] and that he expects to go back to Sri Lanka at one point." Therefore, if Anupa becomes a New Zealand citizen, he said he would definitely obtain Sri Lankan dual citizenship as well. Anupa's example also verifies the fact that his desire to get Sri Lankan dual citizenship is not based on any instrumental benefit Sri Lankan citizenship will provide him; instead, he desires to continue being a Sri Lankan citizen at heart.

Malathi, a female Sinhalese New Zealand resident said her interest to obtain Sri Lankan dual citizenship is also non-instrumental. She said being a Sri Lankan at heart is superior to being a Sri Lankan in a document.

Answering a hypothetical question as to what she would do if she had to choose one citizenship at the expense of the other (Sri Lankan or New Zealand), Malathi decided to go for New Zealand citizenship. She said:

"[Loosing Sri Lankan citizenship would be] the saddest thing ever…[But] that's okay … taking away my Sri Lankan citizenship is like just paperwork. But, from my heart, my body and everything, I [will be] a Sri Lankan… I will keep that identity, being a Sri Lankan, and a proud Sri Lankan."

Anupa's and Malathi's statements suggest that, both consider their patriotic attachment to the home country to be deeply rooted and that there are no alternatives to replace it. They do not believe having access to better instrumental benefits as a host country citizen will affect their patriotic sense of belonging to the home country as home country citizens.

Even many Tamils, some of those who even became victims of the civil war and ethnic discrimination, showed a strong sense of belonging to their homeland. Shiva (60), a male Tamil New Zealand citizen, revealed that he expects to obtain Sri Lankan dual citizenship very soon because he needs to continue his sense of belonging to Sri Lanka. Shiva left Sri Lanka in 1987 due to the ethnic issues. Haunting memories of the ethnic issues did not prevent Shiva from erasing his sense of belonging to the homeland. He said, it is because Sri Lanka is the place he was born. Even though none of his family members wants Shiva to return to Sri Lanka from New Zealand, he strongly thinks he should go back to the land where he was born.

Another example is Conscila, a female Tamil Australian citizen who was directly affected by the civil war in Sri Lanka. She came to Australia in 1995 as a refugee. She said, she could not live in her "own house," in her "own land," because of the bombings and the shootings. Even though this might suggest her entire view towards Sri Lanka to be negative, conversely, she calls Sri Lanka as her "mother country." She also opposed being called a dual citizen in Sri Lanka. She firmly thinks the term dual citizen is inappropriate to identify herself. She said "… when Sri Lanka asks us the dual citizenship, it is very hard. It's a very painful thing for us… We are Sri Lankans. We are very happy to say that we are Sri Lankans."

Anura, a male Sinhalese Australian citizen, thinks emigrants' sense of belonging to their home country also comes with their memories and attachments with certain geographical, religious or cultural locations in the homeland. For example, he said: "…if you are a Buddhist, you will go to the Ruwan Weli Maha Seya [a Buddhist temple in Sri Lanka], if you are a Christian, it's the Madu Church [A Christian church in Sri Lanka] … Even a person who hates the home country for some reason … there can be such attachments that he/she can't easily be detached from." Anura's comment suggests immigrants' patriotic views towards their home citizenship are also constituted by their bonds with the unique places they visited while growing up. Such places also contribute to people's identity of being a citizen of a society. Anura wishes to obtain dual citizenship since he expects to continue his special bond with Sri Lanka.

Asela, a male Sinhalese Australian citizen and a Sri Lankan dual citizen, perceived losing the citizenship of the country he was born as "a big loss" in his life. Asela said "I … did not obtain Australian citizenship [for a while] with the fear that I would lose my Sri Lankan citizenship. I took [the Sri Lankan dual citizenship] because Sri Lanka is our born country." Asela also revealed a sense of gratitude towards Sri Lanka. His strong sense of belonging also caused this sense of gratitude. Asela continued saying "even though [Sri Lanka] is a poor country, it created us, shaped us. The bond we have with [Sri Lanka] is immense. I did not want to lose it. The only reason is that I had a strong sense of belonging to Sri Lanka."

Asela also thought he receives legitimacy to engage in discussions about Sri Lanka if he is a Sri Lankan dual citizen. By obtaining the dual citizenship, Asela said he could "talk about [issues in Sri Lanka] as a full citizen." Even though he used the term "right" to mean his ability to talk about Sri Lanka, there are no such legal right dual citizenship offers. No emigrant needs to have the dual citizenship to be able to talk about the issues in Sri Lanka. Freedom of expression is a democratic right. However, it can be argued that Asela wanted to get legitimacy for his ability to present opinions about Sri Lanka as a full member of the home society. Asela said, "there is an opinion [in Sri Lanka] that, Sri Lankan people who have left Sri Lanka do not love Sri Lanka." Obtaining Sri Lankan dual citizenship was Asela's counter strategy for such popular opinions against Sri Lankan emigrants.

The above examples suggest that one of the main reasons for participants to obtain Sri Lankan dual citizenship is the keen interest to continue their relationship with the homeland. It is evident that participants, both Sinhalese and Tamil, showed a strong sense of belonging to Sri Lanka. Their relationship with the motherland stems from the fact that it is the place they were born and collected numerous memories since childhood. As explained by some participants, the expectation of continuing their sense of belonging with the land is much deeper than any instrumental based bond.

Sense of belonging to the culture

The third recurrent interest that encouraged participants to obtain Sri Lankan dual citizenship was their belonging to the Sri Lankan culture. Many participants viewed that becoming a Sri Lankan dual citizen is related to maintaining their identity as a Sri Lankan. They also believed that obtaining dual citizenship will allow them to continue their belonging to the home culture. They also viewed that obtaining dual citizenship as a way of expressing their sense of gratitude for the country and the culture that made who they are.

For Malathi, a female Sinhalese New Zealand resident, being able to showcase her Sri Lankan identity is a pride. She said "[I'm] very proud to be a Sri Lankan. because we have a long, 2500-year culture… I am very proud of my country and that I am a Sri Lankan… I think I am lucky to be a Sri Lankan." Anusha also shared the same thought. Anusha, a female Sinhalese New Zealand and a Sri Lankan citizen, said, she always wants to visit Sri Lanka as a Sri Lankan, not as a New Zealander. As a result, she said, she does not want to use the New Zealand passport to go through immigration counters in the Sri Lankan airport. Anusha had to visit Sri Lanka using her New Zealand passport. This is because, soon after she obtained New Zealand citizenship, her Sri Lankan citizenship was ceased. By the time of this visit, Anusha was waiting for her Sri Lankan dual citizenship application to be approved.

Anusha visited Sri Lanka once, during the period she was expecting to get her dual citizenship application approved. She recalled her experience of arriving in Sri Lanka using her New Zealand passport to pass the immigration counters. Anusha reminds she felt "guilty" about using New Zealand passport to arrive in Sri Lanka and she said she still feels "guilty" about it. For Anusha, obtaining the Sri Lankan dual citizenship, on the one hand, was about continuing her Sri Lankan identity and on the other hand, an expression of her loyalty to Sri Lanka.

Dinindu, a male Sinhalese Australian citizen also said that he would like to be recognized as a Sri Lankan. His interest to obtain Sri Lankan dual citizenship was to continue his Sri Lankan identity. Dinindu also talked about his willingness to pass the Sri Lankan identity to his children. He said "I teach my children Sinhalese language. [I also take them] to the temple. I value Sri Lankan citizenship as an honour. One day I would love to be retired and live [in Sri Lanka]." Not only Dinindu but many other participants who are also parents also expressed their commitment to passing the Sri Lankan identity to their children who are living in the host countries. Obtaining dual citizenship for their children was perceived as a means of leading them to hold their Sri Lankan identity.

Nilmini, a female Sinhalese New Zealand citizen from Wellington, also revealed her sense of belonging towards the home culture. Reflecting herself, Nilmini said that she always appreciated the values she received by being a Sri Lankan. Nilmini wants to obtain the Sri Lankan dual citizenship to show her gratitude for the cultural values that made her who she is today. She said "… after 25 years, I am still a typical Sri Lankan. [Sri Lankan culture] taught us to be ourselves, have a few good friends...etc. That is not the Kiwi [New Zealand] culture." She also said "... I love my country [Sri Lanka] and love the values, how we share things, how we go out of the way to help people." Nilmini thinks "[she] can never be a kiwi." She assumes the main reason for her inability to become "a kiwi" is her inability to be adaptive to the host society culture. She repeatedly mentioned how much the home country culture influences her day to day life, as opposed to the host country culture.

Similar to Dinindu, Nilmini also wanted her children to continue their Sri Lankan dual citizenship. This is because she thinks, by leading children to visit Sri Lanka continuously will make them realize the Sri Lankan values. Nilmini said

> "[my children] have some values... But by taking children to Sri Lanka at least once a year, they would start loving [those values more] ...[and] they will pass our [Sri Lankan] roots ... to the next generation ... Through that, we can develop a bond between the younger generation and Sri Lanka. That is why I want dual citizenship."

As explained above, participants' interest to become a Sri Lankan dual citizen was based on non-instrumental reasons. Those non-instrumental reasons were strongly related to their sense of belonging to Sri Lanka. As discussed above, this sense of belonging is mainly towards three components: *the people, the land* and *the culture*. Some participants also viewed their sense of belonging as a combination of these components.

Instrumental interests

Five participants out of the fifty-one mentioned that they have instrumental reasons to obtain Sri Lankan dual citizenship. Participants' instrumental ideas were related to managing property, investing or doing businesses in Sri Lanka. However, it is worth to note that, these five participants also had non-instrumental reasons (sense of belonging to the people, the land and the culture) that accompanied their instrumental interests to become a dual citizen. Therefore, according to data, no participant obtained Sri Lankan dual citizenship solely for instrumental reasons.

Two participants out of five said they need dual citizenship because they have land/property in Sri Lanka. They perceived that obtaining legal rights through dual citizenship makes it convenient to manage land/property. Saranya is an example. Saranya is a female Tamil New Zealand citizen. She said "[I have] my husband's properties ... in Sri Lanka" and to manage those, she said she wanted to obtain the dual citizenship. However, she had other non-instrumental reasons as well. Saranya said she wants to become a dual citizen because "Sri Lanka is our motherland. You can't forget your mother.

mother language, people, everything." Saranya's case suggests that her decision to become a Sri Lankan dual citizen is a combination of both instrumental (to manage her property in Sri Lanka) and non-instrumental (sense of belonging) reasons.

The other three participants said they have instrumental reasons, such as investing and doing businesses in Sri Lanka. For legal convenience, they thought of obtaining dual citizenship. Sachini is an example. Sachini, is a female Sinhalese New Zealand permanent resident who is running a business in Sri Lanka. She said being a Sri Lankan dual citizen makes it easier to get done legal and other administrative requirements. However, she also said it is not only for these instrumental reasons she wants to continue her dual citizenship but because of her sense of belonging. She said "my father lived in Italy for 25 years but never obtained Italian citizenship ... he used to tell me when I was small [that I can never change] where I come from... So, I do not want to change [where I was born.]" This suggests that Sachini has a strong sense of belonging to Sri Lanka because it was her birthplace. Hence, Sachini's case also proves that her decision to become a Sri Lankan dual citizen was not only influenced by instrumental reasons (e.g. running a business) but also by her non-instrumental interests (e.g. sense of belonging to the birthplace).

Conclusion

This study explored Sri Lankan diaspora members' perceptions about obtaining the Sri Lankan dual citizenship. As explained above, participants had more non-instrumental interests (sense of belonging to *the people, the land* and *the culture*) to obtain Sri Lankan dual citizenship than instrumental benefits (own property, invest or do business). Based on these findings, I argue that the Sri Lankan emigrants' perceptions were predominantly different from the opinions of the government which are more instrumental. I thus recommend that the government should pay attention to minimize this disparity between them and the diaspora, in order to make Sri Lankan dual citizenship policy more effective. To do so, I suggest the government to re-discuss its present interest in dual citizenship and to see how they can acknowledge diaspora members' non-instrumental interests.

References

Athukorala, Prema-chandra Jayasuriya, S. (2000). Trade policy reforms and industrial adjustment in Sri Lanka. *The World Economy, 10*(2), 387–404. https://doi.org/10.1111/1467-9701.00278

Atkinson, P., & Silverman, D. (1997). Kundera's immortality: The interview society and the invention of the self. *Qualitative Inquiry, 3*(3), 304–325. https://doi.org/10.1177/107780049700300304

Australian Government. (2014). The Sri Lanka-born Community. Retrieved July 24, 2018, from https://www.dss.gov.au/our-responsibilities/settlement-services/programs-policy/a-multicultural-australia/programs-and-publications/community-information-summaries/the-sri-lanka-born-community

Bartley, A., & Spoonley, P. (2008). Intergenerational transnationalism: Asian migrants in New Zealand. *International Migration, 46*(4), 63–84.

David, A. (2011, February 27). Strict new criteria for dual citizenship. *Sunday Times.* Retrieved from http://www.sundaytimes.lk/110227/News/nws_01.html

Department of Census and Statistics. (2012). *Population and Houses Census, Sri Lanka: 2012.*

Department of Immigration and Emigration Sri Lanka. (2018). Dual citizenship. Retrieved October 20, 2018, from http://www.immigration.gov.lk/web/index .php?option =com_content&view=article&id=299&Itemid=59&lang=en

Department of Immigration and Emigration Sri Lanka. (2019). Implementing free visa scheme for designated countries. Retrieved October 23, 2019, from http://www.immigration.gov.lk/web/index.php?option=com_content&view=articl e&id=332%3Aimplementing-the-free-visa-scheme-for-selected-countries&catid=48%3Aentry-visa&lang=en

Fontana, A., & Frey, J. H. (2005). The interview: From a neutral stance to political involvement. In N. K. Denzin & Y. S. Lincoln (Eds.), *The SAGE handbook of qualitative research* (pp. 695–728). London: Sage.

Gamage, S. (1998). Curtains of culture, ethnicity and class: The changing composition of the Sri Lankan community in Australia. *Journal of Intercultural Studies, 19*(1), 37–56. https://doi.org/https://doi.org/10.1080/07256868.1998.9963454

Gamage, S. (2002). Adaptation experiences of Sri Lankan immigrants and their children in Australia in the context of multiculturalism and Anglo-conformity. In A. Richardson, M. Wyness, & E. A. Halvorsen (Eds.), *Exploring Cultural Perspectives: Integration and Globalization* (pp. 3–29). Edmonton: International Cultural Research Network Press.

Ganeshathasan, L., & Welikala, A. (2017). *Report on citizenship law: Sri Lanka.* Badia Fiesolana.

Government of Sri Lanka. Citizenship (Amendment) Act (1987). Parliament of Sri Lanka.

Government of Sri Lanka. Citizenship Act no. 45 of 1987 (1987).

Government of Sri Lanka. Sri Lankan constitution, 19th amendment (2015). Colombo. https://doi.org/10.1017/CBO9781107415324.004

Guest, G., Bunce, A., & Johnson, L. (2006). How many interviews are enough? an experiment with data saturation and variability. *Field Methods, 18*(1), 59–82. https://doi.org/10.1177/1525822X05279903

Henayaka-Lochbihler, R., & Lambusta, M. (2004). *The Sri Lankan diaspora in Italy: an explorative mapping.* Berlin.

Holý, L., & Stuchlik, M. (1983). *Actions, norms and representations: foundations of anthropological inquiry.*

Howie, E. (2013). Sri Lankan boat migration to Australia: motivations and dilemmas. *Economic and Political Weekly, 48*(35), 97–104.

International Crisis Group. (2010). *The Sri Lankan Tamil diaspora after the LTTE.* Retrieved from https://d2071andvip0wj.cloudfront.net/186-the-sri-lankan-tamil-diaspora-after-the-ltte.pdf

Jayanath, A. (2015). The 19 Amendement and dual citizenship. Retrieved May 24, 2018, from https://www.colombotelegraph.com/index.php/the-19-amendment-dual-citizenship/

Jenkins, R. (2004). Symbolising belonging. In *Social identity* (second, pp. 108–123). Routledge.

Krauss, S. E. (2005). Research paradigms and meaning making: a primer. *The Qualitative Report, 10*(4), 758–770.

Morse, J. M. (2000). Determining sample size. *Qualitative Health Research, 10*(3). https://doi.org/10.1177/104973200129118183

Orjuela, C. (2008). Distant warriors, distant peace workers?: Multiple diaspora roles in Sri Lanka's violent conflict. *Global Networks*, *8*(4), 436–452. https://doi.org/10.1111/j.1471-0374.2008.00233.x

Pingama, A. (2016). Reasons for youth migration in Sri Lanka with emphasis on regular and irregular youth migrants. In *2nd International Conference on the Humanities*. University of Kelaniya, Sri Lanka.

Pinnawala, S. K. (1984). *Sri Lankans in Melbourne: Factors influencing patterns of ethnicity*. Australian National University.

Portes, A., & Zhou, M. (1993). The new second generation: segmented assimilation and its variants. *The Annals of the American Academy of Political and Social Science*, *530*(1), 74–96.

Rajasingham, K. T. (2013). No more direct dual citizenship to Sri Lankans abroad. Retrieved May 23, 2018, from http://www.asiantribune.com/node/62252

Rapley, T. (2011). Interviews. In C. Seale, G. Gobo, J. F. Gubrium, & D. Silverman (Eds.), *Qualitative Research Practice* (pp. 16–34). London: Sage.

Reeves, P. (2013). *The encyclopedia of the Sri Lankan diaspora*. (P. Reeves, Ed.). Singapore: Editions Didier Millet.

Roulston, K. (2010). *Reflective interviewing: A guide to theory and practice*. London: Sage.

Silverman, D. (Ed.). (2011). *Qualitative research* (3rd ed.). London: Sage.

Siriwardhana, C., & Wickramage, K. (2014). Conflict, forced displacement and health in Sri Lanka: A review of the research landscape. *Conflict and Health*, *8*(22), 1–9. https://doi.org/10.1186/1752-1505-8-22

Sriskandarajah, D. (2002). The migration-development nexus: Sri Lanka case study. *International Migration*, *40*(5), 283–307. https://doi.org/10.1111/1468-2435.00220

Statistics New Zealand. (2013). *2013 Census ethnic group profiles: Sri Lankan*. Retrieved from http://archive.stats.govt.nz/Census/2013-census/profile-and-summary-reports/ethnic-profiles.aspx?url=/Census/2013-census/profile-and-summary-reports/ethnic-profiles.aspx&request_value=24750&tabname=Languages spoken&p=y&printall=true

Stein, C., & Mankowski, E. (2004). Asking, witnessing, interpreting, knowing: Conducting qualitative research in community psychology. *American Journal of Community Psychology*, *33*(1/2), 21–35.

Toma, J. D. (2006). Approaching rigour in applied qualitative research. In R. C. Conrad, C.F.; Serlin (Ed.), *The SAGE handbook for research in Education*. https://doi.org/10.4135/9781412976039.n23

UNDP. (2016). *Human Development Report 2016: Sri Lanka*.

Wanasinghe-Pasqual, M., & Jayawardena, P. (2017). Sri Lanka's Illegal Migration: detriment to development. In *International Research Conference, Faculty of Arts*. The University of Colombo.

Wayland, S. (2004). Ethnonationalist networks and transnational opportunities: The Sri Lankan Tamil diaspora. *Review of International Studies*, *30*(3), 405–426. https://doi.org/10.1017/S0260210504006138

CHAPTER 5

TRANSITING INTO THE SINGAPOREAN IDENTITY: IMMIGRATION AND NATURALISATION POLICY[1]

Mathews Mathew and Debbie Soon

Introduction

Debates in Singapore about immigration and naturalisation policy have escalated substantially since 2008 when the government allowed an unprecedentedly large number of immigrants into the country. While the city-state is essentially a migrant society, brought about through nineteenth century British colonial interests, Singaporeans have gained a heightened sense of national identity in the fifty years since independence. Being "Singaporean" is essentially, as in other post-colonial societies, manufactured through a series of founding myths and shared experiences. Founding myths include the meritocratic nature of the society, very different from its surrounding Southeast Asian nations where patronage, racial superiority and corruption are rife, and the importance of a strong state to ensure that the nation is able to survive against all odds (Rodan, 2004). Shared experiences, such as a gruelling education system, life in high rise and exorbitant public housing, compulsory military service for men and the melange of cultural celebrations and cuisine further define Singaporeans' identity.

The fact that identity is amorphous and often only well defined in contact with the "other" is clearly demonstrated in the Singaporean case as new migrants come onto its shores. Despite the fact that many of those who come to Singapore are racially similar - from China and India, and the reality that many local born Singaporeans were themselves in a lineage of migrants originating from these same countries several generations ago, local born Singaporeans have asserted the difference between themselves and the new-arrivals. There is some concern on the part of Singaporeans that this group of newcomers are not loyal to Singapore and do not share the essential characteristics of Singaporeans, particularly their unwillingness to adopt Singaporean norms and values (Yeoh and Lin, 2013; Chong, 2015). Rather, new immigrants are sometimes known to show contempt to Singaporeans and refuse to shed markers of their former nationality.

---

[2] This chapter is a reprint of an article originally published in *Migration Letters*. Mathew, M., & Soon, D. (2016). Transiting into Singaporean identity: Immigration and naturalisation policy. *Migration Letters*, 13(1), 33-48.

This essay will discuss immigration and naturalisation policy in Singapore and the tensions that have been evoked, and how these policies are a key tool in regulating the optimal composition and size of the population for the state's imperatives. It will demonstrate that although the state has, as part of its broader economic and manpower planning policy to import labour for economic objectives, it seeks to retain only skilled labour with an exclusive form of citizenship. Even as the Singapore state has made its form of citizenship even more exclusive by reducing the benefits that non-citizens receive, its programmes for naturalising those who make the cut to become citizens which include the recently created Singapore Citizenship Journey (SCJ) are by no means burdensome from a comparative perspective. However some of the additional tightening in recent years is a reflection of the need to shore up continued public support for immigration in the midst of growing strands of xenophobia and to continue manufacturing the ideal citizen.

We begin by outlining the context of discussing immigration in Singapore, before going on to trace the development of naturalisation policy. This essay defines naturalisation as the process of becoming a citizen, and hence, some discussion on the nature of Singapore citizenship is in order to inform an understanding of naturalisation policy.

Role of state in regulation

Singapore is often described as practicing a soft form of authoritarianism. While democratic elections are held, only one party, the People's Action Party has succeeded in forming the government since independence. The success of the PAP has been attributed to its ability to deliver economic and development goals to the nation, a priority which many Singaporeans accept. Election after election, the PAP's track record in keeping Singapore's economy vibrant and shielding it from the full impact of global economic threats, allows it to return to power with few opposition parties making inroads. In order to maintain its hegemony on the Singaporean psyche, the party has not only captured the nation's political and civic discourse but also wields substantial control over individual lives. Through directing how people live their lives, although often intrusive, allows it to achieve its economic objectives and thereby maintain its power base. An important regulatory mechanism that the Singaporean state wields is over the make-up of its population. In Foucault's (2003) writing on governmentality this is described as "biopower"

> "a technology which brings together the mass effects characteristic of a population, which tries to control the series of random events that can occur in a living mass, a technology which tries to predict the probability of those events (by modifying it, if necessary), or at least to

compensate for their effects. This is a technology which aims to establish a sort of homeostasis, not by training individuals, but by achieving an overall equilibrium that protects the security of the whole form from internal dangers" (Foucault, 2003: 249).

Immigration has been a key tool in this framework, in drawing and retaining skilled labour to the country with its exclusive form of citizenship (Vukov, 2003). Unlike in other polities where immigration and naturalisation are the consequence of fairly random events such as war, persecution or economic opportunity, in post-independence Singapore it has been the result of careful planning to ensure the survival of the economic miracle that the ruling party so desires to perpetuate in order to remain in government.

Attracting foreign talent to Singapore's shores

The nation of Singapore has always been acutely aware of its small size and lack of natural resources, which feeds into the often repeated narrative of vulnerability and survival (Chan, 1971). The narrative that human capital is the country's only natural resource often emerges in national speeches, where much has been invested over the years in the education system to ensure that its people are quality labour, with good skills sets to attract investors and global companies to its shores. Singapore has for at least two decades been mindful of the need to draw in skilled labour for it to compete on the global stage. In light of falling birth rates, the state has utilised the tool of immigration to ensure that it has sufficient skilled labour to compete in the global market (Low, 2001).

In 1997, the doors to immigration were opened in the National Day Rally when Prime Minister Goh Chok Tong articulated Singapore's crucial need for new immigrants:

"Gathering talent is not like collecting different species of trees from all over the world to green up Singapore. It is more difficult but absolutely crucial to sustaining Singapore over the long term. Singapore depends on a strong core of talent, in business, government and politics. We need this core, to be an exceptional country and to operate the way we do - rational, forward looking, adaptable. Without this, we cannot run a clean and efficient government, build a professional and credible SAF, run a disciplined police force, train engineers to do R&D, or produce bankers, businessmen, entrepreneurs, managers.

"Because we are exceptional, we have become a key hub in the region, for goods and services, and for capital. This gives us influence beyond our physical size, and translates into a high standard of living.

To produce for world markets, and to be a successful knowledge-based economy, we need intellectual capital. In the information age, human talent, not physical resources or financial capital, is the key factor for economic competitiveness and success. We must therefore welcome the infusion of knowledge which foreign talent will bring. Singapore must become a cosmopolitan, global city, an open society where people from many lands can feel at home." (Goh, 1997)

New immigrants from around the world, described by Prime Minister Goh as "foreign talent" would allow Singapore to be globally competitive, and make the transition to becoming a knowledge-based economy. Even before this there were programmes like the Professionals Information and Placement Service and the Committee on Attracting Talents to Singapore (Singapore Parliament Reports, 18 March 1981; Singapore Parliament Reports, 18 March 1983). However the 1997 speech saw the government pitting Singaporeans against the foreigner who was described as essentially more "talented" and less encumbered by the relative success that was apparent in Singapore. For instance in observing the need for Singapore's national carrier, Singapore Airlines to recruit its star flight crew from outside the country, the Prime Minister remarked that his fellow Parliamentarian,

"Charles Chong, an SIA engineer and MP for Pasir Ris GRC, says that when he travels by SIA, he knows immediately which girls are Malaysians and which Singaporeans. The Malaysians fold blankets better. They do it at home, whereas the Singaporeans get maids to do it for them." (Goh, 1997)

The image of the able foreigner who was crucial for Singapore's competitive edge was further illustrated through the Prime Minister's discussion of soccer matches. As he aptly prognosed:

"Talent makes all the difference...And in football, for the S-league, every club has 5 foreign players. Without them, the quality of the teams would be much lower, and few fans would watch the games. In 1994, the Singapore team had local born Fandi Ahmad as striker. But without Abbas Saad and the other foreign players, we might not have won the Malaysia Cup. In the World Cup, no foreign players are allowed. So apart from countries like Brazil, Argentina, Uruguay, Germany or Italy which have naturally strong players, the others don't really have a chance. Singapore will never have a chance, unless Romario (Brazil), Klinsman (Germany) and a few others like them become Singapore citizens." (Goh, 1997)

The National Day Rally Speech in 1997 pointing to the great need for Singapore to compete in the increasingly competitive Asian environment marked the start of a concerted push to bring in more immigrants, and this most recent wave of immigration. Initiatives to draw skilled labour in included the creation of the International Manpower Division within the Manpower Ministry, which oversees Contact Singapore offices that have been set up in global cities to attract competent individuals to work in Singapore (Ho, 11 November 2000). The attempt to invite skilled labour to Singapore was an overwhelming success. Its outreach efforts and its skilful positioning during the global financial crisis allowed Singapore to draw in a very large number of foreign professionals. In 2007 alone it recorded an increase of 19% of non-resident foreigners on the island. Two years later, there was an 11% increase in those who were granted permanent residency. Singapore's comparative advantage in attracting desirable immigrants is based on its population's cultural affinity with those in East Asia and South Asia, its economic success, low taxation rates and high levels of safety and public order. Table 1 shows how the resident population size has increased dramatically over time, even as fertility rates have been on the decline, and below replacement levels.

Table 1. Singapore Resident Population, 1970-2014 (in thousands)

Population	1970	1980	1990	2000	2010	2013	2014
Total Population[1,2,3]	2,074.5	2,413.9	3,047.1	4,027.9	5,076.7	5,399.2	5,469.7
Resident Population[2,3]	2,013.6	2,282.1	2,735.9	3,273.4	3,771.7	3,844.8	3,870.7
Singapore Citizens	1,874.8	2,194.3	2,623.7	2,985.9	3,230.7	3,313.5	3,343.0
Permanent Residents	138.8	87.8	112.1	287.5	541.0	531.2	527.7

Source: Department of Statistics, Singapore. Population Trends 2014, p.v.

Notes: [1] Total population comprises Singapore residents (i.e. Singapore citizens and permanent residents) and non- residents.

[2] Data for 1970 and 1980 are based on de facto concept (i.e. the person is present in the country when enumerated at the reference period). Data for 1990 onwards are based on de jure concept (i.e. the person's place of usual residence).

[3] Data from 2003 onwards exclude residents who have been away from Singapore for a continuous period of 12 months or longer as at the reference period.

The exclusionary nature of Singapore citizenship

The efforts of the state were targeted at bringing in labour at all levels, from the high to low skilled (Yeoh & Lin, 2012). Lower skilled labour such as what is needed in construction, domestic caregiving and manufacturing are however not accorded an immigration status which will allow them to be ultimately naturalised. They are not permitted to bring in their families or start new ones with Singaporeans. Their residence in the country is tied to their employer's needs. This differential eligibility for naturalisation restricted to highly skilled immigrants, is congruent to the state's intentions to get the best and brightest to remain in Singapore. The state views low skilled migration as transient and makes no effort in retaining this category of labour as citizens (Yeoh, 2006; Yang, 2014).

Besides skill level, naturalisation is also tied with racial background. Singapore practices a hard form of multiculturalism where the state preserves particular racial identities through language recognition policies, quotas in housing allocation and in political representation. Chinese, Malay and Indian identities form the core of Singapore's cultural policies. The state has maintained that to ensure social stability it is necessary that the citizen population maintain the current racial composition achieved by the middle of the nineteen century with a 75% Chinese majority, 13% Malay, 9% Indians and a 3% catch-all, "Others". This has meant that there are quotas in place (although not made official) for the number of new immigrants who are granted permanent residency in the country. In recent years, for instance, the state has noticed its difficulty in attracting those of Malay origin to settle in Singapore partly because Bumiputera policies in Malaysia provide substantial benefits to Malays which they will lose if they accept Singaporean citizenship. Specifically, Minister in the Prime Minister's Office Grace Fu (2013) said in Parliament that *"We recognise the need to maintain the racial balance in Singapore's population in order to preserve social stability. The pace and profile of our immigration intake have been calibrated to preserve this racial balance."*

The exclusionary nature of citizenship is also apparent in the disallowing of dual citizenship and through the means of scholarship criteria. In recent years, the Singapore citizenship has been made even more exclusive by means of the reduction of social benefits for non-citizens.

No option of dual citizenship

The suggestion of dual citizenship has surfaced multiple times in policy discourse, but the state continues to disallow such an option. Discussions of dual citizenship often touch on offering that option to local born citizens, but only threads that address immigration will be discussed in this paper. The suggestion of dual citizenship has been mooted so that immigrants will be more likely to naturalise and socially integrate: *"...allowing dual citizenship will enable us to attract more foreigners to take up citizenship, particularly when we have only 1.26 fertility replacement rate."* (Member of Parliament Leong Horn Kee, Singapore Parliament Reports, 8 March 2004).

"Sir, it can be argued that immigrant dual citizenship facilitates integration into our community by encouraging them to naturalise. By doing so, they share in the cause of Singapore, and feel a psychological and emotional stake in Singapore's progress, beyond the material benefits." (Member of Parliament Irene Ng, Singapore Parliament Reports, 10 November 2006).

However, so far, the option of dual citizenship has not been implemented for the view that Singapore is a young and small nation, and creating a situation of divided loyalties would spell trouble for the country. This is a narrative that has been consistent through the past two decades as pointed out by the government:

"Mr Speaker, Sir, the Government does not allow Singapore citizens to have dual citizenship.

Singapore is a young nation. We have not reached the stage of nationhood where a Singaporean with a second citizenship would still retain his identity and loyalty to Singapore as his homeland wherever he goes, his second citizenship being only of secondary importance.

Foreigners are granted Singapore citizenship only if they are committed to making Singapore their home, and see their long-term future with Singapore, in which case they should readily be prepared to give up their foreign nationality." (Minister of State for Home Affairs Associate Professor Ho Peng Kee, Singapore Parliament Reports, 8 March 1999).

When skilled labour does commit to Singapore in the form of taking up citizenship, it would also entail buying into an exclusive form of formal national identity. Dual citizenship is disallowed, which would require any naturalising citizen to give up their former citizenship. Dual citizenship here acts as a mechanism that selects for individuals who would agree to an exclusive form of national identity and loyalty, at least in the legal sense of being a citizen.

Retaining skilled labour in Singapore

The clear intent of anchoring foreign talent to Singapore can been seen in narratives which touch on the fear that skilled labour may be in Singapore to better their chances of facilitating migration to greener pastures. This includes discussions on medical professionals like doctors and nurses who practise and gain registration in Singapore to better their chances of gaining employment in countries like the United States, Australia, and the United Kingdom (Singapore Parliament Reports, 16 March 1973; 23 January 2007). The stepping stone phenomena also applies to foreign academics and students. Suggestions of the role of Singaporeans in creating a greater sense of belonging, so that these skilled immigrants would feel a connection and want to remain in Singapore have been raised in the policy discourse (Singapore Parliament Reports, 21 November 2005):

"On the issue of foreign students and academics who have temporarily made Singapore their home, they have made a commitment - maybe a temporary one - but I think it is the responsibility of our community and our universities to make them feel as comfortable and to develop as strong a sense of belonging as possible. If we do not do so, they will use our universities as a stepping stone for greener pastures. But since they have made this temporary commitment, I think that we should give them the same ability and the same sense that they can participate, analyse and criticise national issues as well as issues within their discipline." (Dr Geh Min, Nominated Member of Parliament, Singapore Parliament Reports, 21 November 2005).

As a result, the state has made deliberate attempts to keep skilled labour in Singapore at several key points. It does this through the medium of government scholarships to non-Singaporeans, some of which require these individuals to take up Singapore citizenship in the process of completing their scholarship (Singapore Parliament Reports, 28 February 2005; A*Star Graduate Scholarship, 2015).

In a similar vein, Senior Minister Goh Chok Tong said in 2010 that the government was "going to approach some of them [permanent residents] to take up Singapore citizenship. If they don't, then their PR will not be renewed". He further said that out of some 500,000 PRs in the country at that point, *"maybe 50,000 can be selected to become Singapore citizens, the rest can be PRs contributing to the economy"* (Chang, 9 September 2010). A clarification on the statement was issued soon after PRs reacted on online forums, that *"the figure of 10 per cent….was only for illustrative purposes. It is not a target, nor is it the case that all PRs who turn down the offer of Singapore citizenship would not have their PR status renewed"* (Chang, 9 September 2010).

It is clear from a review of policy discourse that the state employs a strategy of both using formal instruments in the form of scholarships as well as persuasion in its strategy of managing the flow of skilled labour in its population.

Reducing benefits for non-citizens

The state has also moved to widen the gap between the social benefits that citizens and permanent residents receive, and in effect, creating a more exclusive form of citizenship. This had been in response to the public sentiment that skilled labour could receive the benefits that citizens could, without any of the obligations and burdens of citizenship. This section of the paper will take a look at the public and state discourse surrounding this development.

There had been the sentiment that many local born Singaporeans bear a disproportionate amount of the obligations of citizenship whilst receiving nearly the same amount of benefits as permanent residents (Hussain, 24 October 2009; Koh et. al., 2015).

This sentiment of inequity plays out especially with the perennial bugbear that new citizens beyond a certain age, as well as permanent residents do not have to perform national service, but that local born Singaporeans bear this burden.

Many public officials have then sought to reinforce the notion that immigration is for the benefit of all Singaporeans, in order to build popular and continued support for the inflow of skilled labour. In a speech to local university students that touched on immigration and population issues, Singapore Prime Minister Lee Hsien Loong said:

"But in the midst of all this discussion about Singaporeans and non-Singaporeans, I think I should emphasize one point. And that is that in Singapore, the interests of citizens always have to come first. Not a short term interest but the long term interests of Singaporeans. And this immigration policy is to benefit Singaporeans in the long term, rather than to benefit non-Singaporeans at the expense of Singaporeans. It is to safeguard our long term interests that we need a sustained and a calibrated inflow of immigrants. But to make quite sure that there is no misunderstanding, we make a clear distinction between citizens and permanent residents and between PRs and non-residents. So when we have budget packages, CPF top ups and so on, they are reserved for citizens. And among citizens, those who have done or who are doing NS will get more than those who have not. And if it comes to public housing, education and healthcare subsidies, we distinguish clearly between citizens and PRs. And I think people know this." (Prime Minister Lee Hsien Loong at the Nanyang Technological University Student Union Ministerial Forum, 15 September 2009).

The state's discourse has relied heavily on pointing out that immigration policies work for the long term interests of Singaporeans, although in the short term Singaporeans may feel the strain owing to the large number of migrants.

To clearly signal however that there is always a distinction between Singaporeans and foreigners, the state has also set out measures to provide differential subsidies whether it is with regards to Government-paid maternity leave and the Baby Bonus for new Singaporean citizen births.

The notion of "benefits" here corresponds to what is described as "rights" in most western liberal democracies. The government sought to reduce the social benefits that non-citizens would get in areas which include education, housing and healthcare. It also ensured various initiatives to recognise Singaporean contributions to national defence through the National Service Recognition Award that sees a sum of money (between $9500 and $10500) deposited into their Central Provident Fund and Post-

Secondary Education accounts over a 10 year period. The various schemes would not only provide differentiation between Singaporeans and non-citizens but also the necessary nudge for permanent residents who have been in Singapore for some time to more fully commit to Singapore in renouncing their citizenship status from their countries of origin and becoming Singapore citizens.

Bringing new citizens into the fold

In the backdrop of issues of social integration, the government established the National Integration Council (NIC) in April 2009 comprising individuals from the people, private and public sectors to tackle the issue (National Integration Council, 26 April 2015). In September 2009, the NIC set up the Community Integration Fund (CIF) that Singapore-based organisations can apply to use to bring about programmes that facilitate the social integration of migrants. To facilitate the process of naturalisation, the state implemented the Singapore Citizenship Journey (SCJ) in 2011, so that new citizens would become acquainted with the history, norms and values of the country. Such attempts in Durkheimian fashion bring about social integration through invoking key symbols and narratives

The SCJ stands as a key bridging point where aspiring citizens are introduced to the national symbols, values and institutions of Singapore. The presentation of the content of the SCJ would mean that when aspiring nationals become citizens, they will be able to participate in and connect with key symbols and narratives invoked in events like the annual celebration of the country's independence.

All citizens that naturalised after 2011 are required to undergo this journey as part of the process of becoming a Singaporean. The SCJ consists of four key components of an online component, a tour of historical landmarks and national institutions, a community engagement session, and culminates in a citizenship ceremony. From the comparative perspective, the requirements of the Singapore Citizenship Journey (SCJ) are not onerous. There are no compulsory language or citizenship quizzes, like in many receiving countries. The amount of time required to complete the citizenship journey is rather minimal, compared to some of the civic integration courses in other countries (Naturalisation, a better passport, 2011). There is even the deliberate effort to frame the SCJ as a rite of passage, or "journey" for new citizens.

Through the historical tour and online component of the SCJ, key national symbols and institutions are presented to aspiring citizens. The online component presents codified content on Singapore's "history and development as a country, key national policies, Total Defence, as well as…[the country's] efforts in building a cohesive and harmonious society" (National Integration Council, 2015b). The tour of Singapore's major historical landmarks and national institutions present physical symbols of Singapore's history and how the country "overcome[s] national challenges in the different domains of urban planning, transport, water resources, as well as security and defence" (National Integration Council, 2015b).

The third component sees aspiring citizens interact and engage with representatives and leaders from the community, which include appointed Integration and Naturalisation Champions (INCs), as well as grassroots leaders. It is described that new citizens will "learn how they can actively participate in the community", and that these community leaders will *"share their experiences living in a multi-racial and multi-religious society, and provide valuable information to help new citizens better settle into their community"* (National Integration Council, 2015b).

The Singapore Citizenship Journey culminates in a citizenship ceremony at the community or national level (National Integration Council, 2015b). A speech is usually made by a state official, which works as a mechanism for bringing new citizens into the fold of the national narrative, is the manner in which state officials frame naturalised citizens as very much part of the history of an immigrant nation, where they are simply the latest to arrive on Singapore's shores:

> "Being a Singaporean has its benefits, but also its obligations. While you enjoy the privileges of a citizen, you also have a responsibility to contribute to your country, Singapore. Singapore, as you well know, is a small country. It has no natural resources like an abundant supply of land or oil; its primary resource are its people. It is the people who built up Singapore, with their drive, hard work, entrepreneurship and frugal habits. These were the values of our immigrant forefathers and I believe you share these values too. Without the will and hard work of its people and leaders, Singapore would not succeed. Singapore today is, of course, better off than 50 years ago, but for it to continue to be better off for you and your children, we will have to work harder together as one united people, whatever our race and religion, and regardless of where we grew up. (Emeritus Senior Minister Goh Chok Tong at the National Citizenship Ceremony 2013).

Key national values are communicated to new citizens at these citizenship ceremonies, which also serve as an opportunity for new citizens to demonstrate their alignment with them. Multiracialism, Singapore's variant of dealing with diversity sees the recognition and protection of four official racial groups of Chinese, Malay, Indian and Others. Multiracialism, as a national value is reflected in policy areas like public housing (ethnic quotas), political representation, and the celebration of national and community level events (Chua, 2007). New citizens are in the citizenship ceremony, required to verbally demonstrate their commitment and resonance with national values through the recitation of the National Pledge, and singing of the national anthem.

"We are a multi-cultural and multi-religious society. This diversity is what makes Singapore unique and we must celebrate this diversity. We must continue to strengthen the social cohesion that we have worked so hard over the years to build. We must continue to embrace and uphold the shared values that make us Singaporeans. When we recite the Pledge later, I hope that you will reflect upon what the words mean to you" (Minister for Manpower Gan Kim Yong and Adviser to Chua Chu Kang Grassroots Organisation, at the National Citizenship Ceremony 2010).

New citizens are also included in major national events, such as the country's 50th year of independence. These key historical points present opportunities for the state to delve into the traits that it is central to the success and story of Singapore, and to invite new immigrants to be a part of this tradition:

"Next year, we will celebrate our 50 years of independence. It has been an amazing and outstanding journey of nation building. It has very few parallels. Our Pioneer Generation dared to think big, make immense sacrifices, stay united and reach for the stars.

They worked hard to overcome the hardships during the early years to build modern Singapore. They lived and worked alongside one another, even though they were of different races and culture, spoke different languages and practised different religions. Over the years, they forged strong and lasting friendships across racial and religious communities. They treated one another with mutual respect, forged a strong community spirit and together built a common Singaporean identity, with a common vision for a better Singapore.

As a result, today we enjoy a strong economy, quality homes and an excellent health care system. We live in a peaceful country, raising our children in a safe environment with many opportunities for them to realise their full potential.

Our Singapore story is a story about individuals putting the society above self, and coming together to collectively build an endearing home for all. As PM Lee Hsien Loong put it in his National Day Rally, it is now our responsibility to continue and build upon their legacy. He called on all of us to be "the pioneers of our generation". As new citizens, you too can do your part, and make your contributions.

Each of you has a unique story and you can make your own individual contributions to Singapore. Some of you are already contributing to the lives of our fellow citizens through the work that you do." (Minister for National Development Khaw Boon Wan, at the National Citizenship Ceremony 2014).

The citizenship ceremony also presents the opportunity for the state to communicate to naturalising citizens the behaviours that it views as desirable. The call to integrate into the community is made repeatedly:

"Singapore is particularly proud of its inter-racial and inter-religious harmony. Against the many racial and religious conflicts elsewhere that we read about daily, the state of affairs here is truly extraordinary. We must treasure it. We must not take our peace and harmony for granted. It requires every one of us to continue to preserve what is important to us - our social harmony; mutual respect for each other; and graciousness when sharing common spaces. We will also need to impart the values that we hold dear to our younger generation so that Singapore remains the peaceful and harmonious country that our Pioneer Generation had painstakingly built. Our ability to rise above our differences will define us, and reflect a Singapore society that is mature and progressive.

As new Singaporeans, you can play your part to reach out to those who have newly arrived on our shores and help them understand our customs and norms as you are better able to understand the challenges they face adjusting to a new environment. At the same time, you should continue building lasting relationships and widen your networks with your fellow Singaporeans." (Dr Yaacob Ibrahim, Minister for Information, Communication and the Arts and Grassroots Adviser at the National Citizenship Ceremony 2011).

Another theme that clearly emerges is how aspiring naturalised citizens are encouraged to volunteer in the community, and that those who do have been held up as exemplars in a very public manner in citizenship ceremonies:

"I would also like to share the example of Mr Ooi Leong Chai, a gardening enthusiast who grew up in Malaysia. He became a Singapore citizen in 2009 and has been very active in the Community Garden Interest Group of Whampoa South Residents' Committee. Mr Ooi takes leave from work to host and interact with students on learning journeys to the RC garden. He also volunteers with the Citizen on Patrol team and joined RC members to promote and help put up the State Flag for residents in the estate during the recent National Day period. Mr Ooi is a good example of an active citizen who believes in being involved in the community." (Dr Yaacob Ibrahim, Minister for Information, Communication and the Arts and Grassroots Adviser at the National Citizenship Ceremony 2011).

The call for citizens to contribute can be read as a policy balancing act, in response to the public sentiment that new citizens and permanent residents do not bear the burden of responsibilities that local born citizens do, as described earlier in this paper.

Conclusion

Citizenship scholars have written about challenges to the ability of national governments to control labour and capital flows (Sassen, 1996). In the Singaporean case immigration and naturalisation policy are very much tools in the government's belt of managing its population for broader state objectives that include economic growth. The state has sought to, with an exclusive form of citizenship, encourage skilled labour to remain in Singapore.

While in many European countries there are reservations about implementing overly prescriptive regimes to dictate the character of immigration flows, the Singapore case illustrates how a nation state can pursue the course of selecting ideal migrants to supplement its projected labour needs. However expecting these immigrants to transit smoothly into a new identity as Singaporeans by giving up their previous citizenship and accept their responsibility to defend the nation is understandably not uncomplicated.

The Singaporean government has been realistic about the demands it can place on prospective new citizens. It recognises that the high skilled candidates it is pursuing for naturalisation have many more options internationally which may be more appealing. As such the Singapore Citizenship Journey and other requirements for citizenship have not been onerous – they are light touches which are meant to facilitate a basic appreciation of Singaporean values and ideals as well as an avenue to cultivate the kind of citizenry the state desires. These requirements most importantly seek to demonstrate to local born and bred Singaporeans that the citizenship process seeks to communicate to new citizens important national narratives.

While the naturalisation process for immigrants that make the cut is not overly demanding, Singapore state leaders expect that over time new Singaporeans and their children who grow up in Singapore will develop a sense of national identity. There is at least some reason to expect this - Singapore's unabashed construction of the "imagined community" through media and public education channels is pervasive. However the extent that state discourse will be able to shape identities might be a naive supposition on the government's part when considering new waves of migrants. With China and India playing a part as dominant world powers and them extending their reach to the global diaspora from their respective nations, there is little guarantee that new citizens from these countries will not continue to feel a strong affinity to their countries of origin. The outcomes of governmentality in managing its population plays out less clearly for Singapore when it comes into contact with similar intentions of the governments in sending countries. In all likelihood, naturalised citizens and even second-generation immigrants will continue to maintain multiple identities and a connection with their sending country. It may be much more realistic for Singapore to merely expect that naturalised citizens and second-generation immigrants will feel enough of an emotional connection to Singapore that will allow them to do their best to contribute substantially to the well-being of the city state.

References

Agency for Science, Technology and Research (2015). "A*Star Graduate Scholarship," Accessed 27 April 2015, http://www.a-star.edu.sg/Awards-Scholarship/Scholarships-Attachments/For-Graduate-PhD-Studies/A-STAR-Graduate-Scholarship-Singapore.aspx

Chan, H. C. (1971). *The Politics of Survival 1965-1967*, Singapore and Kuala Lumpur, Oxford University Press.

Chang, R. (2010). "PRs Won't Be Forced to Become Citizens." *The Straits Times*, September 9, 2010. Accessed April 22, 2015. https://global.factiva.com.

Chong, T. (2015). "Stepping stone Singapore: the cultural politics of anti-immigrant anxieties." In *Migration and Integration in Singapore: Policies and practice*, edited by Mui Teng, Yap, Gillian Koh and Debbie Soon, Routledge, 214-229.

Chua, B. H. (2007). "Multiracialism as Official Policy: A Critique of the Management of Difference in Singapore." In *Social Resilience in Singapore: Reflections from the London Bombings,* edited by Norman Vasu, Singapore, Select Publishing, 51-67.

Department of Statistics, Singapore (2014). *Population Trends 2014*. September. Accessed August 21, 2015. http://www.singstat.gov.sg/docs/default-source/default-document-library/publications/publications_and_papers/population_and_population_structure/population2014.pdf.

Durkheim, E. (1995). *The Elementary Forms of Religious Life*, New York, The Free Press, Simon and Schuster.

Foucault, M. (2003). "Eleven, 17 March 1976." In: *"Society Must Be Defended": Lectures at the Collège de France, 1975-76*, edited by Mauro Bertani and Alessandro Fontana, translated by David Macey, 239-264. New York: Picador.

Fu, G. (2013). "Speech by Ms Grace Fu, Minister in the Prime Minister's Office, Second Minister for the Environment and Water Resources and Second Minister for Foreign Affairs at the Parliamentary Debate on Population White Paper", 5 February. Accessed 21 August 2015 http://www.nptd.gov.sg/portals/0/news/Min%20Grace%20Fu%20Speech%20_Final.pdf

Gan, K. Y. (2010). "Speech by Mr Gan Kim Yong, Minister for Manpower and Adviser to Chua Chu Kang GROs, at the National Citizenship Ceremony 2010", 18 September. Accessed 26 April 2015. https://app.nationalintegrationcouncil.org.sg/Portals/0/Docs/National_Citizenship_Ceremony_2010_Speech_by_Mr_Gan_Kim_Yong.pdf

Goh, C. T. (1997). "National Day Rally Speech 1997: Global City, Best Home." Accessed 15 April 2015. http://www.moe.gov.sg/media/speeches/1997/ 240897.htm

Goh, C. T. (2013). "Speech by Emeritus Senior Minister Goh Chok Tong at the Naitonal Citizenship Ceremony", 31 August. Accessed 26 April 2015. http://www.nptd.

gov.sg/ portals/0/news/esm-national-citizenship-ceremony-2013-speech.pdf

Ho, A. (2000). "Is S'pore Inc Doing Enough to Help Foreigners Settle In?" *The Straits Times*, November 11. Accessed April 22, 2015. https://global.factiva.com.

Hussain, Z. (2009). "Mind the Gap between the Pink and the Blue." *The Straits Times*, October 24. Accessed April 22, 2015. https://global.factiva.com.

Ibrahim, Y. (2011). "Speech by Dr Yaacob Ibrahim, Minister for Information, Communications and the Arts, and Minister in-charge of Muslim Affairs, Grassroots Adviser and Member of Parliament for Moulmein-Kallang GRC, at the National Citizenship Ceremony 2011, 4 September 2011, Accessed 22 April 2015. http://www.nptd.gov.sg/portals/0/news/Speech%20by%20Dr%20Yaacob%20Ibrahim%20at%20NCC%202011.pdf.

Koh, G., D. Soon, and M. T. Yap (2015). "Introduction." In: *Migration and Integration in Singapore: Policies and Practice*, edited by M.T. Yap, G. Koh, and D. Soon, 1-24. Abingdon, Oxon, United Kingdom: Routledge.

Lee, H. L. (2009). 15 September. "Transcript of Prime Minister Lee Hsien Loong's speech at the NTU Students' Union Ministerial Forum, Prime Minister's Office, Accessed 22 April 2015, http://www.pmo.gov.sg/mediacentre/ transcriptprimeminister leehsienloong%E2%80%99sspeechntustudents%E2%80%99unionministerialforum

Low, L. (2001). "The Political Economy of Singapore's Policy on Foreign Talents and High Skills Society." December. Research Paper Series, National University of Singapore Faculty of Business Administration. Accessed 20 April 2015. http://research.nus.biz/Documents/Research%20Paper%20Series/rps0136.pdf

National Integration Council (2015a). "About NIC." Accessed 25 April 2015. http://app.nationalintegrationcouncil.org.sg/AboutNIC.aspx

National Integration Council (2015b). "Singapore Citizenship Journey." Accessed 25 April 2015. https://app.nationalintegrationcouncil.org.sg/ Singapore Citizenship Journey.aspx

Naturalisation a Passport for the Better Integration of Immigrants? (2011). Paris: OECD.

Rodan, G. (2004). Transparency and Authoritarian Rule in Southeast Asia: Singapore and Malaysia. London: Routledge.

Sassen, S. (1996). Losing Control? Sovereignty in the Age of Globalization. New York: Columbia University Press.

Singapore Parliament Reports. (1973, March 16). Budget, Ministry of Health. Parliament No.:3, Session No:1, Volume No.:32, Sitting No.:17 Accessed April 21, 2015. http://www.parliament.gov.sg/publications-singapore-parliament-reports.

Singapore Parliament Reports (1981, March 18) Budget, Public Service Commission. Parliament No.:5, Session No.:1, Volume No.:40, Sitting No.:9. Accessed April 21 2015. http://www.parliament.gov.sg/publications-singapore-parliament-reports.

Singapore Parliament Reports (1983, March 18) Oral Answers to Questions: Expatriates. Parliament No.:5, Session No.:1, Volume No.:42, Sitting No.:9. Accessed April 21 2015. http://www.parliament.gov.sg/publications-singapore-parliament-reports.

Singapore Parliament Reports. (1999, March 8). Oral Answers to Questions: Singapore Citizens Taking up Dual Citizenship, Parliament No.:9, Session No:1, Volume No.:70, Sitting No.:2 Accessed April 21, 2015. http://www.parliament.gov.sg/ publications-singapore-parliament-reports.

Singapore Parliament Reports. (2002, October 1). Motions: Stayers and Quitters. Parliament No.:10, Session No:1, Volume No.:75, Sitting No.:8 Accessed April 21, 2015. http://www.parliament.gov.sg/publications-singapore-parliament-reports.

Singapore Parliament Reports. (2004, March 8). Debate on Annual Budget Statement. Parliament No.:10, Session No:1, Volume No.:77, Sitting No.:5 Accessed April 21, 2015. http://www.parliament.gov.sg/publications-singapore-parliament-reports.

Singapore Parliament Reports. (2005, November 21). National University of Singapore (Corporatisation) Bill. Parliament No.:10, Session No:2, Volume No.:80, Sitting

No.:14 Accessed April 21, 2015. http://www.parliament.gov.sg/publications-singapore-parliament-reports.

Singapore Parliament Reports. (2006, November 10). Debate on the President's Address. Parliament No.:11, Session No:1, Volume No.:82, Sitting No.:4 Accessed April 21, 2015. http://www.parliament.gov.sg/publications-singapore-parliament-reports.

Singapore Parliament Reports. (2007, January 23). Oral Answers to Questions, Public and Private Healthcare Institutions (Number of foreign nurses) Parliament No.:11, Session No:1, Volume No.:82, Sitting No.:8 Accessed April 21, 2015. http://www.parliament.gov.sg/publications-singapore-parliament-reports.

Singapore Parliament Reports. (2009, May 29). Debate on President's Address, Parliament No.:11, Session No:2, Volume No.:86, Sitting No.:6 Accessed April 21, 2015. http://www.parliament.gov.sg/publications-singapore-parliament-reports.

Singapore Parliament Reports. (2010, March 4). Budget, Prime Minister's Office. Parliament No.:11, Session No:2, Volume No.:86, Sitting No.:19 Accessed April 21, 2015. http://www.parliament.gov.sg/publications-singapore-parliament-reports.

Singapore Parliament Reports. (2010, April 27). Benefits for Citizens and Permanent Residents. Parliament No.:11, Session No:2, Volume No.:87, Sitting No.:2 Accessed April 24, 2015. http://www.parliament.gov.sg/publications-singapore-parliament-reports.

Singapore Parliament Reports. (2010, March 10). Budget, Ministry of Community Development, Youth and Sports. Parliament No.:11, Session No:2, Volume No.:86, Sitting No.:23 Accessed April 21, 2015. http://www.parliament.gov.sg/ publications-singapore-parliament-reports.

Singapore Parliament Reports. (2011, March 2). Budget, Prime Minister's Office. Parliament No.:11, Session No:2, Volume No.:87, Sitting No.:20 Accessed April 21, 2015. http://www.parliament.gov.sg/publications-singapore-parliament-reports.

Singapore Parliament Reports. (2013, March 7). Oral Answers to Questions: Dual Citizenship, Parliament No.:12, Session No:1, Volume No.:90, Sitting No.:10 Accessed April 21, 2015. http://www.parliament.gov.sg/publications-singapore-parliament-reports.

Singapore Parliament Reports. (2013, March 11). Budget, Ministry of Defense. Parliament No.:12, Session No:1, Volume No.:90, Sitting No.:10 Accessed April 21, 2015. http://www.parliament.gov.sg/publications-singapore-parliament-reports.

Vukov, T. (2003). "Imagining communities through immigration policies." *International Journal of Cultural Studies,* 6(3): 335-353.

Yang, P. (2014). ""Authenticity" and "Foreign Talent" in Singapore: The Relative and Negative Logic of National Identity." *Sojourn: Journal of Social Issues in Southeast Asia*, 2014, 408-37. doi:10.1353/soj.2014.0023.

Yeoh, B. (2006). "Bifurcated Labour: The Unequal Incorporation of Transmigrants In Singapore." *Tijdschrift Voor Economische En Sociale Geografie*, 97(1): 26-37.

Yeoh, B., & Lin, W. (2012, April 3). Rapid Growth in Singapore's Immigrant Population Brings Policy Challenges. Retrieved September 25, 2014, from http://www.migrationpolicy.org/article/rapid-growth-singapores-immigrant-population-brings-policy-challenges/

Yeoh, B., and W. Lin. (2013). "Chinese Migration to Singapore: Discourses and Discontents in a Globalizing Nation-State." *Asian and Pacific Migration Journal,* 22(1): 31-54.

CHAPTER 6

NARRATIVES OF TRAUMA ACROSS GENERATIONS OF PONTIC GREEKS AND THEIR IMPACT ON NATIONAL IDENTITY

Georgia Lagoumitzi

In place of an introduction: A 'collective amnesia'?

In the eighty years that followed the 1922 Asia Minor catastrophe, the dominant foreign policy interests in Greece imposed a kind of 'collective amnesia' regarding the history of Hellenism in the East (The Balkans, Constantinople, Asia Minor, Cappadocia and the Pontus) on the one hand, and a determination to frame Modern Greek identity along the vector of similarity and continuity on the other. Apart from scholars such as Octave Merlier[1], Richard Clogg[2] or Paschalis Kitromilides[3], few others ventured into the subject of the Greek diaspora in the East. We could even argue that the subject was 'officially neglected'. This neglect aimed at cultivating a sense of continuity of Greek history. This artificial continuity has been especially promoted through school (primary and secondary) reading texts and history books from which any sense of 'diversity' within the Greek borders is absent. Characteristically, one of the post-civil war primary school Readers states: "If we carefully follow the history of the struggles for our country's liberation, we will be convinced of the natural and uninterrupted historical unity from beginning to end."[4] The traditional educational ideological constructs such as "the diachronic presence of the national group in historical time, the uniqueness, self-reference, cultural homogeneity, the glorious historical past" survive until today (Vouri, undated, p. 31). The instruction of history "remains 'trapped' in the national idea, it is treated as a tool for the diffusion of national ideology and identity building and continues to offer dated historical knowledge about the diachronic presence of the nation, cultivating a national consciousness that is ultimately a construct" (p. 33).

The *leitmotif* of the 'undivided unity' of the nation proves a strong

---

[1] "Le dernier hellénisme d' Asie Mineure. Introduction au catalogue de l'exposition (1974)

[2] 'The Bible Society in Pontos: A note concerning the activities of the British and Foreign Bible Society in the Eparchy of Khaldia during the early nineteenth century', Arkheion Pontou, 28 (1966-1967) 161-166

[3] Kitromilides, Paschalis (ed.) *Exodus*, a five-volume work published by the Center for Asian Minor Studies, Vols. 1-5 (1980-2016). Kitromilides edits vols. 3-5 that refer specifically to the 'exodus' of Greeks from various locations within Pontos.

[4] The extract is taken from a history reader aimed for the students of the sixth year of primary school and is subtitled "The historical unity of Hellenism" in Mariolis, D. (2013)

ideological tool in the imposition of the 'collective amnesia'. Yet, contrary to this view that treats identity as an already accomplished fact...we should think, instead, of identity as a 'production', which is never complete, always in process, and always constituted within, not outside, representation" (Hall, 1990 p. 222). Indeed, in the case of Pontic Greeks, we find ourselves before an "ethno-regional identity in-the-making" as Maria Vergeti defines it. According to her, this is the identity of a social group, "member of a wider nation that experiences mass migration from its birthplace without the possibility of mass return. Its identity is not national or ethnic because the group is part of a greater nation and it is not simply regional because the geographical reference space is lost" (Vergeti, 1994 p. 57). Yet, this identity which is tied to the trauma of displacement and genocide encountered many difficulties in "finding acceptance as true history and a valid 'national memory'" (Sjöberg, 2017 p. 4). From 1925 to the early 1980s, the challenge to the narrative of uninterrupted continuity makes its appearance in sporadic commemoration events and publications. Vlasis Agtzidis records the first such event in Western Macedonia (Kozani) already in 1925 while he documents further 'interruptions' in the linear memory that State policies try to impose, from the turbulent 1940s to the 1980s when the issue of genocide and the name of Pontos assumes a wider meaning to include all refugees after the exodus of the Christian population from Asia Minor in 1922 . As Sjöberg states, the background for this change of policy was provided by Greece's transition from traditional authoritarianism to cultural and political pluralism after the Restoration of Democracy in 1974 which "had profound repercussions in national historical culture as the dominant state narrative was challenged by alternative readings of the past" (p. 11). Yet, the path of the "right to memory" has not been a smooth one. Challenges to it continue until today and they reflect not only the different internal, national and partisan narratives but also the workings of factors such as Greek foreign policy in the context of Greek-Turkish relations. Nowhere is the ambivalence of the Greek state in addressing the traumatic experiences and articulate the discourses of Pontic diaspora[5] more evident than in the national debate about the Pontic genocide. In the following section, we present this debate that affected the way in which, not only diasporic identity was re-constructed on

---

[5] The Pontic diaspora was the result of successive migrations of the Greeks of the Pontus region of the Ottoman empire between the years 1916 and 1924. Following extermination and expulsion from their historical home in the eastern half of the southern coastal area of the Black Sea, Pontian Greeks settled in Russia. After continuous internal fermentation and forced migrations, the distribution of the Greek diaspora within Soviet territory became significantly transformed. After 1917 these transformations are divided into three periods: The first period starts with the 1915 genocides of Pontic and Armenian populations in the Ottoman Empire and ends with the final withdrawal of the Greeks from Asia Minor after 1922. The second period focuses on the persecution and exile of ethnic Greeks organized by the Stalinist regime in 1937-1938 and 1941-1944 and culminates in the displacement of the entire Pontic population of Caucasus to Kazakhstan in 1949. Finally, the last wave of migration is associated with the collapse of the Soviet Union. In Lagoumitzi, G. (2011) 25-26

the basis of identity and the recognition of trauma, but also the way in which modern Greek national identity incorporated this new recognition.

The post-2000 Reconstruction Effort: From 'amnesia' to recognition.

As Agtzidis notes, "the ethno-regional Pontic identity is formulated subsequently and becomes more pronounced during periods of democratic euphoria…It is only then that the descendants of those often opposite local groups of the 1920s and 40s will unite in one common historical narrative that is centered in an idealized memory of Pontos and its culture while after a process of change and transformation it will ultimately focus on the memory of genocide" (Agtzidis et.al., 2010 pp. 199-200). The ideological changes and transformations referred to at this point, concern the divisions and fermentations within the different Pontic groups regarding the problem of genocide. On the one hand, the group on the left of PASOK (Panhellenic Socialist Movement) pushed for the recognition of genocide in the Pontus, which was suppressed by imperialist forces like Turkey. [6] On the other, Right wing Pontic groups were echoing the position of the Greek Right, according to which demands for the recognition of the Pontic genocide were untimely (Agtzidis et.al. 2010, p.263). However, during the Second World Congress of Pontic Hellenism in1988, the two groups agreed to advance the genocide agenda, thus raising the issue into a major policy matter for the Greek State. It is only after 2000 that a serious effort to bring historical trauma to the frontstage was attempted. The decisive event which rekindled the interest in the history of this side of Hellenism was the 'homecoming' of 150,000-170,000 Pontic Greeks from the ex-Soviet Union, a process that spanned from 1989 to 1997. It seems to have been the necessary condition for ending what has been interpreted as the 'conspiracy of silence'. [7] The history of Pontic Hellenism in the Soviet Union which remained largely unknown until the late 1980s began to be researched, narrated, and documented.

The past speaks through memory, narrative and myth and only over the past 30 years have we started to listen. It was then that collective trauma made its appearance as a meaningful cultural frame for the socio-historical debates that followed. According to Alexander and Breese, such traumatic narratives "create powerful, history-changing effects in the worlds of morality, materiality and organization" (2013, p. ix). Moreover, they affect diasporic identities and through them, the identity of a nation. Finally, they "trigger significant repairs in the fabric of a society" (p. xii) but also create new challenges or indeed "new rounds of social suffering" (Alexander, 2012, p.

---

[6] Vlasis Agtzidis attributes the formulation of the demand in these terms to the influence of Dependency theorists such as Samir Amin on Left wing groups.

[7] "Gia to zitima ton Pontion" *Socialist Change*, 13 (1990) found in Agtzidis, et.al. 2010, p. 267)

2). This study focuses on the above dimensions and, based on refugee narratives, seeks to present the impact of reconstructed meanings on official policy. It also recognizes the fact that substantial cultural work is required before individual narratives of suffering become translated into collective trauma. For example, I have shown elsewhere how the Greek Parliament recognized the 19th of May as the day commemorating the Pontic genocide in 1994 as "the culmination of the Pontic groups' struggle to 'the right to memory' (Lagoumitzi, 2011). More recently in 2017, a monument dedicated to the Pontic Greek genocide was unveiled. Such sites reinforce what Micieli-Voutsinas calls 'affective heritage' which "mobilizes embodied experiences in relation to memorial dogma to produce a kind of 'feeling truth' for visitors. This is especially true at sites commemorating traumatic pasts" (2016, p. 2).

However, the institutionalization of traumatic memory has continued to be challenged until today. Two parliamentary Bills, 2193/1994 and 2645/1998 are related to the process of the institutionalization: the former recognizes the 19th of May as Remembrance Day for the genocide of the Pontic Greeks while the latter, the 14th of September as National Remembrance Day of the genocide of the Asia Minor Greeks by the Turkish state. It was the first time that the Greek state directly accused Turkey for genocidal intentions and their execution by an army organized by the Neoturks and Kemalists, thus acknowledging a national trauma.

Shortly after the unanimous vote of the Greek parliament, a 2001 Presidential decree removed the term 'genocide' from the parliamentary Bill that had been passed three years before (1998) recognizing the genocide of the Asia Minor Greeks. The term had been replaced with 'catastrophe'. It is clear that this was the result of a campaign launched by a number of political parties, which were rejecting the term either for fear of encouraging 'nationalistic' sentiments or fear of complicating Greece's foreign relations with Turkey. One of the latest 'acts' of this controversy appeared on the pages of a number of Greek-American newspapers[8] and involved ex-minister of education Nikos Filis and Thea Halo, author of "Not Even my Name"[9]. Halo's book provides a unique adaptation of her mother's experiences of persecution and flight until she reaches her destination, America. It is unique because she provides evidence of the genocide from the perspective of the victim and because it is the only English-language account of this sort. In fact, it could also be viewed as an effort to internationalize or 'cosmopolitanize' the genocide narrative of the Pontian diaspora. (Sjöberg,

---

[8] Halo, T. (2015, November 5) "From Thea Halo to Members of the Greek Parliament" Hellenic News of America, 5, Retrieved from: https://hellenicnews.com

No author (2015, November 6) "The Ignorance of Education Minister Filis on Genocide" The National Herald Retrieved from: https://www.thenationalherald.com

[9] Halo, T. Not Even My Name: A True Story 2000. (New York: Picador)

2017 pp.156-186). In an open letter to the Greek Parliament, Halo defended the term 'genocide' while asking for the resignation of the minister of education. At the same time and in line with the new Left wing government's educational policy for the year 2015-2016, the chapter on Black Sea Hellenism in the 19th and 20th centuries was removed from the core curriculum of the history textbooks in the senior year of the high school. [10] This decision by the Greek ministry of education was defended on the grounds that such chapters were filled with 'nationalistic' overtones. Once again, the field of education had turned into a ground of controversy over nation, collective identity, and reconciliation. Collective trauma in Greek history has always been constructed through partisan conflict and the case of Pontic Hellenism was no exception. The Greek Parliament during the years 2015-2018 did not stop at the negation of the term Pontic genocide, but, as the diaspora newspaper *efxinospontos.gr* reports, "for a second time in a row, during the special plenary session of the parliament, the parliamentary Chair himself announces the celebration of the National Remembrance day of the Asia Minor catastrophe, not of the genocide of the Asia Minor Hellenism by the Turkish state, as law 2645/1998 requires".[11]

As Coddington and Voutsinas assert, "narratives and discourses highlight how the complicated and emotional politics of truth surrounding traumatic experience are social and relational, embedded not only in the individual psyche, but also in the wider body politic" (2017, p.53). Yet, far from harboring 'nationalistic' overtones, diasporic collective memory frameworks, culture, rituals, and collective commemorative representations, "promote another heritage that "de-essentializes the nation and the 'totalizing' political ideologies that accompany it" (Lagoumitzi, 2011, p. 10). As such, diaspora history is not only vital in breaking what has been called 'the conspiracy of silence' (McKinney, 2007), but it also makes accessible "past sources of belonging [that] can endure in a virtual sense through the act of nurturing the connection in memories and can be used to 'warm up' and give vitality to the present" (May, 2017, p. 401). The exploration of these two functions of diasporic memory will be the focus of the next section.

Individual trauma, traumatic narratives, and their reconstruction as socio-cultural frames

Our methodology is informed by the turn to memory studies, a field that was 'discovered' three decades ago and continues to be vibrant and

---

[10]   Ministerial   Decree   96080/Δ2/17-6-2015   (Government   Gazette   B'   1186) https://www.slideshare.net/sambrin1971/1186-2015-2015-16 The chapter by Konstantinos Fotiadis: "The Hellenism of the Black Sea" in Topics in Modern Greek History (undated) Diofantos pp. 223-270) has since been reinstated.

[11] "The suppression of the term genocide and its substitution by the Parliament with the term Catastrophe constitutes an affront to the Asia Minor Greeks" efxinospontos.gr (17 September, 2017)

productive. Oral historians embraced memory as "a source for 'people's history'" (Thompson, 2007, p.50). Haunted by the exclusion of the experiences of historical subjects such as important working-class actors, social historian Paul Thompson tried to demonstrate that "oral history was transforming both the content of history-.... by bringing recognition to substantial groups of people who had been ignored- and the processes of writing history..." (Thompson, 2000, pp. 25-81). Thus, memory as the subject and the source of oral history is thought to offer a unique insight into individual and collective experiences. Eyerman captures this reality in the following assertion: "memory provides individuals and collectives with a cognitive map, helping orient who they are, why they are here and where they are going (2004, p.4). What is at stake here is the way in which individual experiences of suffering are translated into collective representations of such afflictions. In this context, traumatic narratives are the means through which these symbolic worlds emerge in authentic Husserlian tradition: that is, both synchronically and diachronically, immediately and in a temporal way. Memory 'maps' individual *lived experiences* as social and cultural phenomena and therefore calls into question 'easy' distinctions between the objective and subjective, the individual and the collective, memory and history. As Spector states, "...the goal of "intimate story" itself is to do away with these dichotomies [internality/externality, in/out, a structure of identity and alienation] or to render senseless the segregation of the most private experience from public narratives of peoples and politics" (1998, p. 35). As is evident from the discussion, what becomes of cultural representations of individual traumas is also a matter of 'performative power'. "The production of memory is a performative practice, and inevitably social" (Edkins, 2003, p. 54). "...Effective performance depends upon more than creating powerful symbols. It is a matter also of material resources and demographics, which affect, even if they do not determine, what can be heard and who might listen" (Alexander, 2010, pp.2-3). This was discussed earlier in the debate on 'genocide' regarding Pontic Greeks. Indeed, the understanding of the use of such 'typifications' is of great importance since they reflect the social forces and cultural meanings that helped produce them. In the narratives of trauma, the uses of terms like genocide, catastrophe, displacement, exile and nostalgia reflect not only different individual experiences, but also defining moments in the making of distinct generations as 'communities of memory' (Bellah, 1985, p. 153). It is important also to recognize the shift of focus that is implied here from the individual to the collective level. As Olick maintains, "the fact that memory of such personally traumatic experiences is externalized and objectified as narrative means that it is no longer a purely psychological matter" (Olick, 2007, p. 32). Pontic Greek narratives are important not only as accounts of personal suffering but rather as legitimating frames of our history and identity, of how we define ourselves.

They live on long after the death of the last survivor of the Asia Minor catastrophe, or the Stalinist forced exile of the Greeks from Caucasus to Kazakhstan or Siberia. Collective memory studies reveal the processes through which identities are constructed.

Karl Mannheim's sociology of generations: Narratives and generations

In the search for identity through collective memory we cannot bypass Karl Mannheim's sociology of knowledge and 'the problem of generations'. (1928/1952) Arguing against both, a positivistic and a romantic-historical understanding of generations, Mannheim opts for a third, sociological reading. He writes: "while the nature of class location can be explained in terms of economic and social conditions, generation location is determined by the way in which certain patterns of experience and thought tend to be brought into existence by the *natural data*[12] of the transition from one generation to another" (1928/1952, p. 292). He thus introduces a unique perspective on the dynamic development of social relations, social knowledge and social action. Simple generational separation performed by positivist demographers on the basis of simple biological facts is rejected as meaningless. Instead, he defines a generation in terms of distinct collective experiences of given age groups, which stamp those age groups with a permanent separate identity. These experiences, in turn, give a new meaning to both, individual (subjective) and historical (objective) time. Moreover, Mannheim distinguishes between the generation location, actual generations comprised of individuals bound together by a common destiny, and 'generation units' the latter being different or even antagonistic groups within the same actual generation. Even though they might be different, they are oriented toward one another (pp. 306-307). In this way, he intimates the dialectical relationship between history and knowledge. Individuals are determined by the historical processes that were dominant in their youth and resulted in the formation of historical/actual generations. Their biographies are shaped by their positioning in history and their participation in the events of their time.

The conceptualization of diaspora as a 'narrative of displacement' provides the opportunity to assess the impact of such traumatic experiences on successive generations of Pontic Greeks. Sharing the experience of successive displacements from the Ottoman Empire to Russia (1914-1924), from Caucasus to Kazakhstan (1937-1939 and 1941-1949) under the Stalinist regime, and finally from the ex-Soviet Union to Greece in the wake of the 1989 Revolutions, they constitute an ideal-typical group for the study of the

---

[12] Italics in the original.

way in which different generations perceive a common past.

The advantage of Mannheim's generational approach is its diachronic character, or what Corsten calls 'polyphonically organized time perspectives' (Corsten, 1999, p. 267). Mannheim's theorization of the generational problem is clear and takes us beyond the spatial location and historical experiences that characterize each generation. The new element here is the time dimension. What follows is an exploration of generations of Pontic Greeks through narratives of trauma, everyday struggle, and achievements. From twenty life-story interviews conducted over a two-year period (2013-2015) and one unpublished memoir[13], there emerge two generations of Pontic Greek refugees. Based on the meanings that interviewees' themselves attribute to their experiences, I detected two generations, the 'displaced' and the 'frustrated' generation.

The major theoretical assumptions based on the sociology of generations that we set out to explore were the following:

1. What is the meaning of trauma for various generational groups? What is the role of emotions in the process of remembering?

2. To what extent is a generation a product of memory?

3. What new theme (s) demarcate a new generation given that "the decisive tribute for an emerging generation is that it gains acceptance for introducing a new theme, and thereby transforming the structure of the intergenerational discourse?" (Corsten, 1999, p. 268)

There is little doubt that during the interviews with members of the two distinct generational groups, we were confronted with narratives of trauma. Based on our research of historical generations, it was anticipated that traumatic memories and experiences would be more pronounced among members of the 'displaced generation', that is among those who, as children or young adolescents experienced the Stalinist purges of 1937-38 and/or whose families were exiled to Kazakhstan from 1941 to 1949. They were between 72 and 77 years old when they arrived in Greece.

This group has a strong sense of being victims of a 'double genocide', first in Pontos and then in Stalin's Soviet Union. They were still carrying memories of their parents' persecution by the Young Turks in Pontos and their flight to pre-revolutionary Russia. However, what seems to shape their identity further is their experience of persecution as 'enemies of the state' and 'anti-revolutionary' elements by Stalin's regime. Iakovos Lavrentiadis

---

[13] I am grateful to Dr. Vlasis Agtzidis for making this unique memoir available to me. Iakovos K. Lavrentiadis "The Odyssey of a Refugee from Pontos" (Aspropyrgos, 1993)

compares their fate to that of the 'collectivization' victims of 1929-1933 (Unpublished memoir, 1993). They also see themselves as victims of corrupt 'external forces', alluding to the impersonal, bureaucratic mechanisms of a totalitarian regime that ruined the lives of people. This generation is marked by memories of successive displacements. This finding substantiates Mannheim's emphasis on the time dimension which in turn, becomes the definitive moment in the capturing of generations. Aboim and Vasconcelos elaborate further on this old Mannheimian theme while adding the discursive dimension. "Generations only exist if, sitting in a given structural location, discourses about one's own time are mobilized for self-identification.... individuals in a given historical time–space may share mental and practical dispositions, but most importantly they must always position themselves in face of the narratives that have become dominant to describe that generation location" (2013, p. 12). Therefore, narratives of genocide, deportation, and exile blend to produce a 'displaced' generation. Moreover, we find ample evidence about the "formative role of memories of historical events from adolescence and early adulthood in the creation of a generational culture" (Misztal, 2003, p. 88)

Some of our interviewees gave us emotionally-charged accounts of the deportations and subsequent exile they endured, while they seemed to be seeking, even after sixty years, some form of closure in the sense of "a resolution which allows the event to become integrated into the psyche" (Klempner, 2000 p. 70). They recounted their inability to understand why those deportations happened and mentioned the confusing state they were in not only on the night of the event, but for years to come. Kostas stated that upon his and his family's arrival in Greece, he started looking around for books that could explain why this happened to his family. "I still don't understand why an eleven-year old child was taken out of bed at one o'clock in the morning to leave for the train station. It was June 13, 1949 a sweet summer night and we had to leave everything behind. We spent twenty-two days on a freight train carrying manure. We had no idea where they were taking us, but most importantly, why. We were given food and water only when the train stopped at the stations. (Kostas, personal communication, February 2015). It is evident that strong emotions of our respondents' experiences were elicited from adolescence through early adulthood and it is those emotions that are constitutive of a distinct generation that survived deportations and exile, and the journey of 'return'[14] to Greece.

---

[14] 'Return' is a figure of speech since in reality the majority of the Pontic Greeks of the former Soviet Union had never been to Greece before. In this sense the term 'repatriation' is used rather metaphorically, yet at the same time, it reflects the reality of that group's motivations and definitions of themselves. As such, it demonstrates the power of narratives. A similar analysis of the question of 'return' to the occupied part of Cyprus of young Cypriots who have never known that part is made by Roudometof and Christou In Eyerman, et.al. (2003, pp. 163-187)

The second generation is identified as the 'frustrated' generation. It includes those who arrived in Greece from 1989 to 1996 as adolescents or young adults. If the previous generation learned to part with everything they had created through time, this generation came to Greece with hope and anticipation of a better future, only to discover prejudice and overt discrimination. In a number of interviews, they stress the feeling of 'nostalgia' and 'worship' for a country they knew very little if at all, which however turned to alienation and frustration. (Alexis, personal communication, September 2015) They speak of themselves as 'strangers in a land they called their own'. (Christoforos, personal communication, May 2014). We could argue here that generations of Pontic Greeks displayed "affective citizenship" which is described by Ayata as the real feelings of a group toward the nation, state or political community, while 'failing' the test of legal citizenship ("where one is really from") upon 'homecoming' (Ayata, 2019: pp. 330-331). In two interviews, there is even mention of 'moral damage' regarding the Pontic Greek identity which was replaced with the demeaning term "Russo-Pontians". (George, Maria and Christoforos, personal communications, June 2014). This they experienced as a 'demotion' as they were often compared by locals with 'gypsies' and Albanians. Identity issues dominated the discussions: "In Russia we were Greeks and in Greece we are Russians" they say. "Our descent is recognized as Greek but not our consciousness". "We were called 'return' migrants which is deliberately misleading for someone who had survived two genocides" (C. personal communication, March 2013). The 'double genocide' issue is still vivid in most of the interviews. There are frequent references to the issue of the official recognition of the Pontic genocide and one can see that this is part of the moral universe of this generation too. As Martha Nussbaum says, "emotions play an essential role in any recollection because memories not tagged by ongoing social emotions tend to fade out, and because emotions are always 'in part about the past' (Nussbaum, 2001, p. 177).

Another source of frustration apart from identity issues is the new refugees' interaction with state bureaucratic institutions which is seen as a 'profanation' of the 'sacredness' of their culture and history. The lack of accountability of state officials, their 'rubber ideology' which can be stretched only as far as the next national elections and the 'blindness' of the new refugees when it comes to their rights constitute only some of the frustrations mentioned. Finally, they report discrimination and 'racist' attitudes that they have to combat at every step. Their integration into the Greek society after twenty-five years since their arrival is still an unfinished project.

Eva Papadatou, European Director of the General Secretariat of Hellenes Abroad has said in a conference titled 'Woman, Pontic, return migrant from the former USSR': "What is distinctive about Pontic Greeks today is that they did not return to Greece for economic reasons, but rather in order to preserve their identity. Despite this however, they suffer like other categories of migrants, racism, xenophobia and social exclusion…"[15]

The 'frustrated' generation is facing several problems, practical and moral. For at least twenty-five years, Pontic Greek generations have tried to expose the problems they encounter mainly through their associations. Recently, certain NGOs have attempted to promote solutions to the more practical problems the new refugees confront. There are multiple issues today that remain largely unresolved for the Pontic Greek population. Matters such as instruction and training, recognition of university degrees and development of social capital, issues of retirement (the acknowledgment of working years in the former Soviet Union) and property issues in their birthplaces. The housing problem in Greece as well as more recent problems generated by the current crisis, more specifically loans, continue to exist. It is clear the Greek government is called upon to address such issues that are pending for decades. On the other hand, there has been considerable progress in the cultural sphere. The promotion of music, dance, theatre by the various Pontian organizations in Greece soon became diffused into the Greek society. Inevitably, the organization of the different refugee waves in influential associations such as *Efxinos Leshi* (1933) or *Panagia Soumela* (1951) in Thessaloniki but also *Argonaftes-Komninoi* (1930) in Athens signaled a change in the visibility of the Pontic Greeks in the realms of culture and history. The work of these and numerous other associations has left its mark on the national consciousness.

Conclusion: Changing the nation?

The exploration of traumatic narratives, their transformation into cultural frames through which diaspora generations and generation units derive their identity has confirmed our initial assumptions about collective traumas and their impact on national identity and the self. Assumptions such as the constructivist and imagined nature of collective traumas seem to be corroborated by our findings. Indeed, "the truth of cultural scripts emerges, not from their descriptive accuracy, but from the power of their enactment" (Alexander and Breese in Eyerman et. al. 2013, p. xxvii).

In this study, I became witness to the powerful enactment of the Pontic genocide as narrative. The different generations that were identified, decades apart from each other, projected the issue as a major identity-building frame. Trauma is an intergenerational phenomenon even though the younger generation may not have direct memory of it. From a psychoanalytic perspective, Faimberg has claimed that this 'tyrannical intrusion of history' is

---

[15] The conference took place in Athens on the 30th September 2015 and was organized by NGO NOSTOS.

an unconscious, narcissistic process. He postulates: "In this kind of identification process, a history is condensed which, at least partially, does not belong to the patient's generation." "The condensation of three generations is what I call 'telescoping of generations'" (Faimberg, 2005, p. 9). In the present findings, far from being unconscious, the narrative of genocide is weaved across generations and within different generation units. Mannheim's generation units are the key to understanding why there are different degrees of consciousness or willingness to highlight such traumatic frames.

Yet, the most important conclusion is that after the end of the 1980s, narratives of trauma gradually found their way into becoming crystallized as collective representational frames through education, commemoration rituals, memorial sites and ultimately through official channels of recognition into Greek history. The linear, uninterrupted narrative of unity of the nation was ruptured. Until recently, we maintained a national history of continuity through agreement that looked to the past. In the future, the challenge will be to embrace continuity through difference. This will require the continuing transformation of the socio-political fabric of the Greek society in the direction of recognition, cultural pluralism, and the socioeconomic integration of new Pontic refugees.

Acknowledgement:

I am grateful to Dr. Leonidas Sotiropoulos for his comments on an earlier draft.

References

Aboim, S. Vasconcelos, P. (2013) "From political to social generations: A critical reappraisal of Mannheim's classical approach" *European Journal of Social Theory*, [no volume number], pp. 1-19 DOI: 10.1177/1368431013509681

Agtzidis, V., Lemonidou, E., Kokkinos, G. (2010) *Trauma and the politics of memory: Some aspects of symbolic wars for history and memory* Athens: Taxideftis

Alexander, J. (2012) *Trauma: A social theory* Cambridge: Polity

Alexander, J., E. Butler Breese (2013). Introduction: On social suffering and its cultural reconstruction. In R. Eyerman, et. al. (eds.) *Narrating trauma: On the impact of collective suffering*" (pp. ix-xxxv) London: Paradigm Publishers

Ayata, B. (2019) "Affective citizenship" In Slaby, J., von Scheve, C. *Affective Societies: Key concepts* London: Routledge pp. 330-339 e-book https://doi.org/10.4324/9781351039260

Bellah, R., et. al. (1985) Habits of the heart: Commitment and Individualism in life New York: Harper and Row

Campbell, J. (1968) Modern Greece New York: Frederick A. Praeger

Clogg, R. (1966-67) 'The bible society in Pontos. A note concerning the activities of the British and foreign bible society in the eparchy of Khaldia during the early nineteenth century', *Arkheion Pontou*, 28, Athens: Epitropi Pontiakon Meleton pp. 161-166

Coddington, K., Micieli-Voutsinas, J. (2017) "On trauma, geography and mobility: Toward geographies of trauma" Emotion, Space, Society, 24 pp. 52-56 Retrieved from: http://dx.doi.org/10.1016/j.emospa.2017.03.00

Corsten, M. (1999) "The time of generations" Time and Society, 8 pp. 249-272

Edkins, J. (2003) Trauma and the Memory of Politics Cambridge: Cambridge University Press

Eyerman, R. (2004) "The past in the present: culture and the transmission of memory" Acta Sociologica,, 47, 159-169

Faimberg, Haydèe. (2005) The Telescoping of Generations: Listening to narcissistic links between generations London: Routledge

Hall, S. (1990) Cultural identity and diaspora. In J. Rutherford (ed.) Identity: Community, culture, difference (pp.222-237) London: Lawrence and Wishart

Halo, T. (2015, November 5) "From Thea Halo to Members of the Greek Parliament" Hellenic News of America, 5, Retrieved from: https://hellenicnews.com

Klempner, M. (2000) "Navigating life review interviews with survivors of trauma" *Oral History Review*, 27, pp. 67-83

Lagoumitzi, G. (2011) The uses of nostalgia in the 'imagination' of diaspora: The case of the new Pontic Greek refugees. In M. David, J. Muñoz-Basols (eds.) *Defining and re-defining diaspora: From theory to reality (*pp. 25-40) Oxford: Interdisciplinary Press

Mannheim, K. (1928/1952) The problem of generations In P. Kecskemeti (ed.) *Karl Mannheim:Essays* (pp. 276-322)) London: Routledge

Mariolis, D. (2013) *National identity and ideology in the history school readers of the 6ᵗʰ grade in the post-civil war period: 1950-1974* "Unpublished master's thesis,

Panteion University, Athens Retrieved from: http://elibrary.iep.edu.gr/iep/articles/article.html?id=33

May, V. (2017) "Belonging from afar: nostalgia, time and memory" *The Sociological Review*, 65 pp. 401-415 DOI: 10.1111/1467-954X.12402

McKinney, K. (2007) "Breaking the conspiracy of silence: Testimony, traumatic memory and psychotherapy with survivors of political violence" *Ethos*, 35, pp. 265-299 DOI: 10.1525/ETH.2007.35.3.265

Micieli-Voutsinas, J. 2016 "An absent presence: affective heritage at the National September 11th Memorial & Museum" *Emotion, Space Society*, 24, 93-104. Retrieved from: https://doi.org/10.1016/j.emospa.2016.09.005

Misztal, B. (2003) *Theories of social remembering* Maidenhead: Open University Press

Nussbaum, M.C. (2001) *Upheavals of thought* Cambridge: Cambridge University Press

Olick, J.K. (2007) *The politics of regret: On collective memory and historical responsibility* London: Routledge

Roudometof, V. Christou M. (2003) 1974 and Greek Cypriot identity: The division of Cyprus as cultural trauma In Eyerman, R. et. al. (eds.) *Narrating trauma: On the impact of collective suffering*" (pp. 163-187) London: Paradigm Publishers

Sjöberg, Erik. (2017) *The making of the Greek genocide: Contested memories* New York: Berghahn Books

Spector, S. (1998) "Edith Stein's passing gestures: Emphatic portraits" *New German Critique*, 75, pp. 28-56

Thompson, A. (2007) "Four paradigm transformations in oral history" *The Oral History Review,* 34, pp. 49-70 DOI: 10.1525/ohr.2007.34.1.49

Thompson, P. (2000). *The voices of the past: Oral history.* Oxford: Oxford University Press.

Vergeti, M. (1994) *From Pontus to Greece: Formative processes of an ethnic-regional identity* Thessaloniki: Kyriakidis

Vouri, Sophia. (Undated) "The instruction of history in the modern political conjuncture" *Theoreio, Paedagogic Currents in the Aegean*, pp. 30-37.

CHAPTER 7

IMMIGRATION AGENTS IN BAHRAIN: AN EXPLORATION OF THE IMMIGRATION POLICY NEXUS

Simeon S. Magliveras

This chapter draws on Gell's notion of agency and nexus to understand transnational Filipino agency is situated in an environment where policies and *de facto* practice limit the choices of the transnational subjects. This chapter demonstrates the complexity with regards to immigration policy and nexus of agents which result is the practice or lack of practice of said policies. By discussing immigration policy in Bahrain, this chapter uses Alfred Gell (1998) seminal work, "Art and Agency" to which the notion of policy nexus presented in the introduction of this volume was sown. Policy is not merely taking care of necessities of work for host/guests, remittances, or GDP needs. This chapter examines agency[1] in immigration policy. Thus "agent"[2] are categorized and obligated to follow and interact with labour policy and regulations. But, the subjects of the policy with alternative intensions or objectives[3] may find the policies antithetical to their needs to which, they act accordingly. In the most general sense, this study examines the nexus between immigration policy and practice. More specifically, this study explores immigration policy nexus of several agents, 1) a guest worker from the Philippines, her cultural background, her life and obligation to home, her obligations to her employer, and 2) her Bahraini employer, the employers obligations to the state, her business, and her family, and 3) the immigration policy itself.

Needless to say, there are many more agents who/which are involved in creation and practice of immigration policy, however, this chapter focuses on

---

[1] Boswell & Hampshire (2017) and Christensen & Laegreid (2009) examines agency from the political science perspective focusing on leaders as agents of policy not considering the other influencers or the subjects of policy. Rapport & Dawson (1998) discuss transnational as free agents not tied to primordial models of place. Neither consider policy or how policy categorizes and creates transnational identities.

[2] Agents, in this case, are any entity or individuals who are linked to the policy. In other words, international organization, governments, employers and employees, etc. could be effected or affect policy. This contrasts with the idea of agency as: This term is linked to sociology which focus on the individual as a subject and view social action as something purposively shaped by individuals within a context to which they have given meaning. 6/27/2020 http://bitbucket.icaap.org/.

[3] This intension may/may not be counter to the intentions understood by the creators of the policy. Thus actions upon those policies may not be illegal but certainly test ethical or moral behaviours at times.

three above mentioned agents on the receiving end of immigration policy[4]. The center of this discussion is Joselin. Joselin is a Filipina working in the service industry. Next, is her employer, Fausia, who owns two salons in Bahrain and one in Dubai, UAE. Finally, there is the policy itself. The policy determines the structures which affects the behaviors of the latter two agents. Successful immigration policies have intensions and must be congruent with the morals of the society (Haines 2013). However, policies are also manipulated to appropriate benefits from workers by those in a more advantageous positions (Shore and Wright 1995). Shore and Wright(ibid.), as well as Haines (2013) suggest this is often the case, however, as seen in this study 'powerful' individuals or entities may use their status to sublimate those same policies to meet alternative objectives.

Behind these agents, Joselin, Fausia, and the policy are also many unseen actor/agents. Though beyond the scope of this particular study, the nexus also includes the policy processes from both from host and home countries, the intensions of the individual's respective cohorts: families, businesses, etc., as well as, their respective cultural backgrounds resulting in consequences far outside the expectations of the policy makers[5].

To begin, it should be clarified that this case study is not suggesting there is a failure in the system. On the contrary, Bahrain is considered a success story not only in the GCC and but globally, which would explains its ranking as a prime destination for ex-pats[6]. Nor does this study suggest Bahrain is an undesirable place to work or live. Rather, this study explores how the immigration policy nexus operates.

Immigration Policy of Bahrain

Bahrain is a constitutional monarchy and a member of the Gulf Cooperation Council[7] (GCC). According to the Mudi Index, the population of Bahrain is 1,442,659 (July 2018 est.) individuals of which 48% are non-nationals (Mudi index 7/29/2020). Employment and migration is closely regulated as is true in all GCC counties. Bahrain uses the Kafala system as a

---

[4] In much of the research the construction and articulation of policy does not examine how policy is actually interpreted approached in everyday life, Voiceless powerless being (Foucault 1977) become the objects of policy (Shore and Wright 1995). Or those subjects are envisaged as free unrestrained actor who do not recognize powerful entities (Rapport and Dawson 1998).

[5] The focus of this study is on the actors who are working within the confines of immigration policy. The creators and enforcers are also salient to policy nexus, however it is beyond the scope of this article.

[6] According to the Internations survey, in 2017 and 2018 Bahrain was considered place world with the best quality of life for ex-pats. (Internations 6/27/2020) In 2019, Bahrain still maintains its position as the most favorable destination for expats in the middle-east, however, it has dropped to 6th place out of 168 countries (Gulf Insider 10/20/2019). Over 20,000 respondents take part in the survey of the 3.6 million Internations members.

[7] The Cooperation Council for the Arab States of the Gulf was originally known as the Gulf Cooperation Council. It is an economic block consisting of Bahrain, Kuwait, Oman, Qatar, Saudi Arabia, and the United Arab Emirates

regulatory system for immigration which has been criticized by both those people in the GCC and human rights advocates (Diop et. al 2015). Bahrain has been proactive in attempting to establish equitable systems for its foreign worker[8]. Interestingly, Bahrain is considered one of the prime destination for foreign worker despite criticism of the Kafala system. Bahrain is also a relatively open society compared to many of its Gulf neighbours. Bahrain touts itself as a place where foreigners can practice their religion freely[9]. There is also a thriving nightlife with movie theaters and clubs. There are social clubs (Nagy 2008) for the different nationalities which cater to the needs of the various immigrant communities. Bahrain is also a relatively small country so access to government service such as health service, labour service etc. are relatively easy to access. Last but not least, Bahrain's cost of living is relatively low[10] and Bahrain is an easy destination for people looking for work from developing counties. Consequently, it is also a favourite destination for Filipinos who are looking for work to support their families at home.

Joselin came to Bahrain because she heard that Bahrain was a place which needed workers, paid well, had a low cost of living, and most importantly, Bahrain was an easy place to get a work visa and permit so that she could

---

[8] Gardner (2010) discusses the different factions pressuring the government to establish policies more equitable for business owners. At the time his work was published, there was a debate to whether employees could change jobs at any time or they would be obligated to wait one year after they began at a new place of work. The 1 year rule work transfer rule became law. He did mention that home citizen groups were lobbying the government to put it into labour policy.

[9] There are many Christian sects and churches, Hindu temples, and even a synagogue.

[10] In the past an employer could solicit employees directly which placed employees into potentially risky situation. According to interviews with manpower companies in Bahrain and in the Philippines, in the last several years there have been regulation put into place to minimize risk. As a result direct hiring is no longer legal. There are two ways in which someone can be hired to work in Bahrain in 2020. 1) A licensed recruitment agency with offices in the Philippines and a sister office in Bahrain will search for a requested position. The person is then hired. They go through a set of seminars prepared for OFW who will travel to the Middle East by the Government called the Philippine Overseas Employment Administration (POEA). According to the website the POEA's function is to: a) Regulate the industry – the main purpose is to set minimum standards and to issue licenses, arbitrate issues between the recruiters and the new employees , b) Employment facilitation – to assist in the preparation of recruits, evaluate contracts and deploy workers to their destination, c) Workers protection – register workers and prepare them through orientation seminars about their destination and finally, d) General administration and supportive services- which is basically fiscal and office management. Philippines Overseas Employment Administration http://www.poea.gov.ph/programs/programs&services.html Retrieved 7/14/2020. The POEA has limited authority once the workers are deployed however. Corresponding recruitment agencies have only ninety days to which their workers can make a complaint about their working conditions or their employer. If major grievances are not resolved then, in theory, the worker is returned to the Philippines. The recruitment agency are then obligated to replace the worker. However, since all the parties will lose there is a tremendous pressure to maintain civility for the first three months. After that the employee is obligated to return all the initial costs to his/her employer which may be difficult to do. 2) The second way to work legally in Bahrain is to visit Bahrain with a tourist visa. This is usually done by visiting a close friend or family member for a few months. Before the tourist visa ends, the individual will find a job and have his/her changed to a worker visa under and the employer agrees to sponsor the new workers visa. This has the added advantage in that the visitor can evaluate the potential new boss and the new boss, sponsor, forgoes costs for the recruiter and initial plane ticket.

support her family.

Joselin's Story

Joselin is one of the estimated 158,644 Overseas Foreign Worker (OFW's) from the Philippines in Bahrain (Department of Foreign Affairs Philippines 7/29/2020). She is 45 years old, married with two children. Her situation is not out of the ordinary. Joselin has been in Bahrain for 14 years. She trained as a beautician in the Philippines. She chose to migrate when her husband abandoned the family. Both of her children are presently going to a private college which would have been too expensive if she had worked and remained in the Philippines. Establishing herself in Bahrain she was able to take care of her aging mother (her father died in 2017[11]). She was given permission to return home but did not take emergency leave because she was concerned about the cost of travel and loss of income while she was not working. In addition, she is putting both her children through school and gave of them all the comforts in life they would not have had if she had remained in the Philippines for work.

Joselin began her life in Bahrain as a nail technician with a neighborhood salon in the capital, Manama. Every few years she moved to better and more prestigious salons. Joselin has been with the same salon for the past 7 years. She was hired to be the floor manager because of reputation for attention to detail. As a floor manager she made the top end of the salary scale which is approximately 450 BHD/month[12]. When she started working in Bahrain, her salary was less than 150 BHD/month. Starting salary for a basic nail technician is approximately 175 BHD/month in 2020. Ex-pats are promised housing, free health care, transport to and from work, and holiday tickets home. The floor mangers are the most important position in the salon. The floor manager is responsible for the ordering of all the products used in the salon. The floor manager is responsible for making sure the tools are all properly sterilized and the shop is clean and presentable to clients. Joselin is also the primary person to deal with clients matters such as quality control, complaints, etc. In addition, she is the first person to deal with employees' issues such as performance, labour, and health, as well as, issues of abuse and/or pilfering. She has to make sure the clients are scheduled properly and that the clients are satisfied. Being the floor manager is sometimes also very alienating. She is has little real authority but is in charge of discipline in the shop and is inevitably blamed by clients, by her employer, and by the other

---

[11] Joselin as many transnationals had a difficult time with the passing of her father. She was far away and did not do to her father funeral and did not take time off from work because she would have missed it. Physical absence seems to be intensified when there is a loss of a close loved one. Madianou (2013) and Parreñas (2005) discuss the physiological trauma that physical distance from family causes.

[12] In the Philippines, she would be making 10000 FP/mo. which is approximately 80BHD/mo.as a floor manager

employees if a conflict are not resolved well. However, she understands that Fausia puts great trust in her. Joselin feels that Fausia and her family is like her own family.[13]

Joselin's problems at work began in 2018, when she had a disagreement with Fausia's daughter about getting holiday off time after Ramadan[14]. Ramada[15] is the busiest time of year for beauty salons. The women work very long hours well into the night. As a result, the workers are given a few days off after Ramadan. However, Fausia had just opened a new salon on the other side of the island and needed a good floor manager to organize the brand new salon. Joselin protested because said she was completely exhausted and felt she needed a few days' rest which indecently, was given to the other women in the salon. Fausia's daughter told her she would get the break after the new salon was established. Finally, after much contestation and some angry exchanges between Fausia's daughter and Joselin, Joselin begrudgedly opened and organized the new salon. However, her relationship to Fausia seems to have changed. Shortly thereafter, Joselin was asked to go to Dubai to train a new group of Filipinas for a new salon Fausia was preparing to open in Dubai. Joselin went to Dubai on a tourist visa. The consequence was problematic. She was working illegally so Fausia had her stay with Fausia's sister and the new employees would come to the house to be trained. She was in Dubai for approximately a month. She never left Fausia's sisters house. Joselin was also promised the opportunity to go to Britain to open a salon there after her work in Dubai was completed. Joselin was told she would wait for her paperwork to go to the United Kingdom in Dubai. The opportunity never materialized. At the end of the month, Joselin was told there was a problem with her paperwork and that they would send her home to the Philippines until things were sorted. She trusted Fausia but by then her work visa in Bahrain had lapsed and that her visa was not renewed because she was out of the country.

With no work visa, Joselin was obliged to return to the Philippines. Fausia told her she could come back and manage the new salon in Bahrain. This meant Joselin would have to reapply from the beginning to return to

---

[13] Mandianou (2013) illustrates the importance of maintaining family ties. Filipinas sometime substitute this longing for family ties with their employers.

[14] Joselin, as is her employer, Fausia as well as Fausia' daughter and even the policy can be considered social agents in this case because they all become a catalyst for a chain of events. Gell (2001) defines agency as "Agency is attributable to those persons (and things) who/which are seen as initiating a causal sequence of a particular type, that is, events caused by acts of the mind, or will, or intension rather than mere concatenation of physical events. An agent "causes things to happen" (Gell 2001:16) Gell continues to suggest that agents' intension and the resulting cause/effect may be different having unintended consequences.

[15] During Ramadan, women want to be beautified for their friends and family because it is a time where families and friends visit one another. Muslims fast during the day and day work hours are reduced. Workers in the salons start later but have to work all night to service their clients.

Bahrain[16]. Fausia told her, she would bring her back as soon as possible. Joselin's flat would be secure and all her things would be safe. Unfortunately, it took over a year to bring her back. She retained her position as floor manager. However, Fausia told her she would not be able to pay her the 450 BHD/month and because of the economic turndown. Fausia would only be able to afford giving Joselin 300BHD/month. In addition, when she returned she was not eligible to receive her 'indemnity[17]' which would have added to 7 months' salary extra paid to Joselin at the end of their contract. What happened? Is Joselin a victim? Why did they let Joselin's visa laps? Moreover, why did Fausia offered her job back and why did Joselin agree to come back under the new conditions?

Before considering these questions, it is important to outline the rights and responsibilities of the employer and employee according to Bahraini Immigration Policy. The employer /employees contract is defined by the kafala system. The regulatory system was developed for guest workers in the Middle East based on an old tradition of patronage and hospitality (Doip et al. 2015). Employer/employee rights and responsibilities are mediated through the Labour Market Regulatory Authority (LMRA), with accordance to the kafala system, the employer has to make a clear contract of obligation from both parties. If agreed upon, the contract binds both employer and employee. The kafala system structures the rights and responsibilities of the employee and his/her rights defining the number of hours worked, pay raises, days off, and the responsibilities the workers have in the work place. In addition, the kafil (or sponsor) theoretically guarantees all costs incurred in preparation for new employment (in other words, the cost of new visas, travel cost to Bahrain, medical exam costs, etc.), the employee health insurance, room and board (or a cash supplement which the worker can use to rent and pay for food), as well as, air-fare to and from home at the beginning and end of contract and holidays which is usually offered once every two years (Magliveras 2019). However, the kafala system by itself has little to no de facto checks and balances, so abuse can occurred on many levels, as a result, there have been attempts throughout the Middle East to ban the kafala system all together (Diop et al. 2015; Johnson 2015). The main issue of abuse is because employers are given a tremendous amount of power[18]. The system

---

[16] Getting permits is a complicated and time consuming bureaucratic process. Work permits are arranged by the employer, but the employee has to have a health exam, verification of criminal records, go through OFW training and have all valid identification and passports.

[17] Indemnity is the term used for the end of contract bonus which is stated in the law as one month's salary per annum to be paid when a worker returns home permanently.

[18] Employers have almost complete power over their employees. If they pay late, or if the employer does not want the worker to take time off, then the employee has little recourse. This especially problematic for house maids/servants who under international law are not covered by international labor laws. There are cases where women are on call twenty-four hours a day and are locked in their rooms

is directly dependent on the good will of the employer (Diop et.al. 2015).

The Labour Market Regulatory Authority (LMRA)

The Labour Market Regulatory Authority was established in 2006 (LMRA law 7/3/2010). The LMR provides services related to employment laws and regulations for expat employees because accurate information is sometimes hard to come by. It is a primary information center which provides expat employees with clear guild lines about all legal matters with regards to labour. The LMRA issues work visas and renewals, transfers from one job to another. It also provides entry visas and residence permits and worker ID cards for workers and their dependents and facilitates medical checkups with the health ministry. In addition, though it does not decide labour disputes directly, the LMRA is the first place to go to in the process to resolve such problems. Official complaints against employers can be made at the LMRA[19]. The LMRA was instituted to deal with issues originating from flaws, "Kafala systems which is one of the most controversial and vexing policy questions facing the region today" (Diop et al. 2015: 116). In Joselin's case, the way she was let go and rehired is dubious at best and the LMRA would have been involved if she had chosen them to. But, it does not explain why Joselin on her return, did not take Fausia to the Labour Market Regulatory Authority (or LMRA)[20] to which she had every right to do. Some things that must be considered to explain the choices of both Joselin and Fausia and why they behaved in the manor they did. Agency is key to the reasons she did not prosecute.

Agency

According to Gell (1998:16) an agent is " Attributable to those persons (and things) who/which are seen as initiation causal sequences of a particular type, that is, events caused by acts of mind or will or intention, rather than mere concatenation of physical events. An agent is one who 'causes things to happen ' in their vicinity". Gell envisages agency not only a cause and effect

---

when the employer's family leave the home as well as sexual abuse (Domi 2019; Human Rights watch 2016; Moore and DeRegt 2008; Seeman and Fischer 2015).

[19] Before the LMRA was created there were mechanisms for dispute resolution but the system was very complicated and workers either did not understand their right or the rights were so limited because the kafala system does not afford them de facto the flexibility to formally complain about working conditions (Marigold 1995, Johnson 2010). Marigold and Johnson discuss the labor relations in Saudi Arabia. In their articles it is clear how one sided the power relations are. An example of the power dynamic is the practice of passport confiscation. In the recent past it was law that a workers passport would be confiscated. In 2009 it became illegal to confiscate an employee's passport. The study found that it is still practiced in Bahrain today by many employers.

[20] The LMRA is the Bahrain system to deal with labour disputes. There are similar such government organs in other GCC countries but with various degrees of success. Bahrain's LMRA is very proactive in assisting ex-pats in their needs in issues of labour law. The LMRA has the mechanisms to petition employers to pay back pay for holidays but also clearly outline the documents required by employees to leave the country legally as well as clear instructions for labour disputes or transfer to other employers.

relationship but one that has intention or the potential to affect others. The agent therefor becomes a place where the potential causation originates. Agents have three characteristics according to Gell (ibid.): 1) causation, 2) result, and 3) transformation

Joselin as agent

From first impressions, Joselin appears to be a victim in this scenario. Joselin is out 7 months bonus pay and has had a deduction in her salary. Joselin needed money to support her children's education and to help her elderly mother. Moreover, the kafala system's structure gives her employer much power in determining her life in Bahrain. Her employer can terminate her employment at any time for any reason and send he back home. Her employer can also black list her for several years so she cannot re-enter the country simply stating that the employee did not hold up her part of the contract.

When Joselin was sent home, she easily found a job for the time she was working in the Philippines. But she had no intension of staying in the Philippines for long. She had friends maintain her accounts with the local mobile phone company and had them pay her debts to the bank while she was away. Joselin could have gone to a manpower agent in Manila and returned on her own at a new job but she did not. She is talented and experienced, and such nail techs can find a job anywhere in the Middle East easily. Joselin had many advantages to going back. However, Joselin actively maintained contact with Fausia and chose to return to work for her even under the lesser conditions. But, why did she go back to Fausia? It is because in many ways Fausia was a good employer. She always was paid on time. She had a prestigious position in a good salon. Joselin was treated like a family member and was invited to family gatherings. Joselin felt she could depend on Fausia if she had problems at home[21]. Going to another employer had risks. She did not know if they paid on time or whether she would be able to take off time if needed. There were many scenarios where she would be even in a lesser advantageous stage if she went to a new unknown employer. In addition, if she was unhappy in the future with Fausia she could find another job in Bahrain once she completed her year back.

In addition, Joselin had much social capital in Bahrain. She was in Bahrain 14 years and had created a loyal client base. She had Filipino and non-Filipino friends, who she could depend on if she needed a favor. Joselin had much more to lose if she were to come back under someone else's sponsorship. As a result, she chose not to go the LMRA to complain and willingly took the pay cut.

---

[21] Fausia helped her pay the expenses such as funeral arrangements etc., after her father's death

Fausia as agency: Narratives of superiority?

Fausia clearly was in a more power position than Joselin. Fausia could have fired her and hired someone in her place. Since she sent her home, she could have simply taken her things and thrown them away. Fausia could have even black listed Joselin which would have made it impossible for her to return to Bahrain. However, she did none of those things. She kept her promise, kept her things and went through employment agencies to make sure Joselin could come back and work for her. But it is peculiar that she acted the way she did. First, taking her to Dubai for a month and letting her visa expire and then bringing her back.

To better understand Fausia's intent, it is important to understand something about Bahrani/Arabian culture, in particular in the Gulf. Gulf society is a very hierarchical (Al Lily 2018). Status is defined by age, profession and gender. Obedience to people in higher statuses is prized (Al Lily 2018). Moreover, Filipinos as other third world people are *de facto*, not given full rights as citizens (Margold 1995). Even though there appeared to be mutual respect between Joselin and Fausia and Joselin was treated as a member of the family, she was not part of the family. It appears that Joselin forgot her place.

Joselin insistence having time off, even though she had the right to take a few days off was seen as an aggressive disobedient act. In addition, her argument with Fausia's daughter was seen as a sign of great disrespect. Moreover, Bahrain is a society where *wasta* (connections) and the patron/client system is deeply rooted in the society (cf. Campbell 1964). Patrons and clients have particular obligations to one another. Fausia saw Joselin's resistance as breaking the rules of the patron/client relationship[22]. Fausia helped her with her father's funeral as well as other less serious situations. From Fausia perspective, she was simply asking Joselin to delay her days off a few weeks. Thus, Fausia created a situation that would reprimanded Joselin. So that Joselin would understand her obligations to Fausia. Fausia wanted her back because she was a good and tough floor manager. The predicament in this case is that the labor policy do not give Fausia the flexibility to reprimand Joselin 'properly'. So the policy had agency. It made Fausia created a scenario to which Joselin understood was for her benefit, instead the whole purpose was to reprimanding Joselin, showing her who was boss. The policy was created envisaging the sponsors

---

[22] Campell (1964) discusses how patron/client systems operate. Clients and patrons have social and 'moral' obligations to one another. There is an exchange of gifts and favors. Patrons need clients just as clients need patrons. Patron need clients to maintain their prestige and status and clients need patrons because they need access to limited resources and power stature not otherwise accessible

as patrons of lesser people[23]. As her patron, Fausia did her a favor by hiring Joselin and being her to Bahrain. The clients debt is not really a monetary issue (Campbell 1964), though it is often put into monetary terms. Thus as patrons, employers expect complete loyalty and ask them to do more than they are obligated by contract to do[24]. Fausia was generally happy with Joselin's work but Joselin forgot her place. So, in Fausia's mind, she had no choice but to send Joselin back to the Philippines. As an agent, Fausia chose to end Joselin's contract and rehire her.

Policy as agent

Objects are not usually thought of as agents. Gell (1998) refers to object agents as patiences. His analysis is extensive. But briefly a patient is an agent that because of it nature has intension and therefore alter others behavior around them. A coffee table is a good example. Placed in from of a settee, it acts as an agent forcing individuals to place their cups of tea and coffee on it. Policy is similar as a patient, it forces people to act in a particular way, to interpret and either to follow regulation or to avoid regulation. Policy categorizes people and they act upon that categorization. Jenkins (2008, 2014) work suggests that by categorizing people they act upon that category whether positive or negative and that category effects the categorized' s identity and behavior. Likewise Shore and Right (1995) point out that policy creates categorized people and these categories are enacted upon. It then, makes the subjects react as they embody those categories (Jenkins 2008). Thus, the immigration policy which defines people as kafils (sponsors) or as guest worker places them into particular categories, defining their obligations to one another. However, the morals (of social hierarchies and obedience) and obligations (to the business and to immediate family) the labor policies in this case, goes counter to the values of the kafil. So the kafil has to create a situation subverting the intension of the policy and the policy as an agent then affects her behavior. Fausia sends Joselin on a wild goose chase. In addition, Fausia understanding of obedience also goes counter to the policy. She chooses to send Joselin home rather than obliging herself to the policy. In Joselin's case, Joselin chooses to continue with Fausia, to not press charges, and to take a cut in salary which is also counter to the policy's intention. The labor policy is a patient agent affects everyone associated with it.

---

[23] Gardner (2010) discuss the debate by Bahraini citizen advocate groups about the limits on ex-pat workers freedoms when establishing their rights to leave a job. He mentioned that discussions about ex-pats having a year obligatory work with a new contracts were being discussed. In 2020 it is law.

[24] The research for this project has seen very few exceptions to the rule. Employees are asked to delay their holidays sometimes for several years, work over time putting their own personal needs on the back burner from sometime whimful employers.

Conclusion

This work illustrates the immigration policy nexus at work. Every actor has a part to play but, it is not that they are passive actors who have unchanging roles in this scenario. They are all agents with limitations but with choices which effects the outcome of others either as patience agents or as direct agents. Fausia and Joselin both chose to work together. In contrast, with a structural/functional model where individuals as part of the system with no choices, they have viable alternative choices. Fausia could have gotten someone else to run her shop. Joselin also could have chosen to come back to the GCC with better pay working for someone else. The LMRA policy is also not a monolithic unchanging entity. Rules evolve as unseen consequences arise, or as old policies no longer apply in new present situations. Thus, they interact and affect one another. Joselin is neither a victim of a hierarchical system in which she has no choices because she comes from a place with less advantages as she chose to stick with Fausia even though she understood the underhandedness of the situation. Nor does she ignore the power structure enabling her to work outside the system (Butler 2005; Kirstoglou 2004). Joselin understands her status in Bahraini society and chose as a return benefitting her family and fulfilling her obligations as a Filipino society understanding her role as an OFW mother and bread winner.

Each has agency as is clear in Joselin and Fausia's case. Policy affords freedoms in various degrees to different people. Evidently the one with fewer choices is Joselin. She, or people less fortunate than her have less choices than their Kafil. Joselin is hired as a technical employee which contrasts greatly with house maids or home nurses who would not fall into the same category as her and they do not have as many rights that she has. Worker in homes are also socially isolated so their choices are even fewer. Their choices in times of crisis or abuse may be either to stay or flee. And many times without proper identification they become fugitives. Foreign workers must maneuver within the immigration policy framework. To conclude this subject on a positive note, it is important to discuss Gell (1998) transformation. What is the transformation? The vast majority of people living and working in Bahrain are 'successful' agents. They have transformed both their home countries and their host countries. As OFW's, they help their families, raise their families quality of life, educate their children and benefit their government with greatly needed foreign currency. They benefit their host lives as well. OFW's help build their hosts economy and give essential services in all levels of society. It is especially clear in these times of the Covid 19 pandemic where the front line is made up of Filipino health workers. Finally consider a thought, guest works become patient agents too. Their success pressures policy makers to create more equitable policies for the workers themselves. Thus, the policy is not a monolithic law either. Policy is a changing thing that is affected by others and at the same time effects others.

References

Al Lily, A. (2018). The Bro code of Saudi culture.

Athabasca University http://bitbucket.icaap.org/dict.pl?alpha=A Retrieved 6/27 2020

Boswell, C., & Hampshire, J. (2017). Ideas and agency in immigration policy: A discursive institutionalist approach. European Journal of Political Research, 56(1), 133-150.

Butler, J. (2005), Giving an Account of Oneself, New York: Fordham University Press.

Campbell, J. K. (1964). Honour, Family and Patronage, a Study of Institutions and Moral Values in a Greek Mountain Community. Oxford University Press, London

Christensen, T., & Laegreid, P. (2009). Organising immigration policy: the unstable balance between political control and agency autonomy. Policy & politics, 37(2), 161-177.

Diop, A., Johnston, T., & Le, K. T. (2015). Reform of the Kafāla System: A survey experiment from Qatar. Journal of Arabian Studies, 5(2), 116-137.

Donini, A. (2019). Social Suffering and Structural Violence: Nepali Workers in Qatar. In Gironde C. & Carbonnier G. (Eds.), The ILO @ 100: Tackling Today's Dilemmas and Tomorrow's Challenges (pp. 178-200). Leiden; Boston: Brill. doi:10.1163/j.ctvrxk4c6.16Gell, A. (1998). Art and agency: an anthropological theory. Clarendon Press.

Gardner, A. (2010). In City of Strangers: Gulf Migration and the Indian Community in Bahrain. Ithaca; London: Cornell University Press. Retrieved July 10, 2020, from www.jstor.org/stable/10.7591/j.ctt7z9b5.11

Gulf Insider "Bahrain, Falls from 1st Place to 6th for Expats" https://www.gulf-insider.com/bahrain-falls-from-1st-place-to-6th-for-expats/ Retrieved10/20/2020

Hampton, Maricar (6 July 2012). Filipinos etching credible mark in Bahrain. FilAm Star. Retrieved 10 May 2019.

Human Rights Watch. (2016). [O]. In World report 2016: Events of 2015 (pp. 433-437). Bristol: Bristol University Press. doi:10.2307/j.ctvndv9bj.21

Internations survey https://www.internations.org/expat-insider/2018/the-gcc-states-39595 Retrieved 6/27/2020

Jenkins, R. (2008). Rethinking ethnicity. Sage.

Jenkins, R. (2014). Social identity. Routledge.

Johnson, M. (2011). Freelancing in the Kingdom: Filipino migrant domestic workers crafting agency in Saudi Arabia. Asian and Pacific Migration Journal, 20(3-4), 459-478. Labour

Kirtsoglou, E. (2004). For the love of women: Gender, identity and same-sex relations in a Greek provincial town. Psychology Press.

Market Regulatory Law Authority Law http://lmra.bh/portal/files/cms/shared/file/law-no19-year2006-english.pdf Retrieved 7/3/2020

Madianou, M., & Miller, D. (2013). Migration and new media: Transnational families and polymedia. Routledge.

Magliveras, S. S. (2019). Filipino Guest Workers, Gender Segregation, and the Changing Social/Labour-Scape in the Kingdom of Saudi Arabia. Migration Letters, 16(4), 503-512.

Margold, J. A. (1995). Narratives of masculinity and transnational migration: Filipino workers in the Middle East. Bewitching women, pious men: Gender and body politics in Southeast Asia, 274-98.

Moors, A., & De Regt, M. (2008). Migrant domestic workers in the Middle East. In Schrover M., Van der Leun J., Lucassen L., & Quispel C. (Eds.), Illegal Migration and Gender in a Global and Historical Perspective (pp. 151-170). Amsterdam: Amsterdam

University Press. doi:10.2307/j.ctt46mwss.9

Mudi Index. Bahrain Demographic Profile 2019 https://www.indexmundi.com/bahrain/demographics_profile.html Retrieved 7/29/2020

Nagy, S. (2008). The search for Miss Philippines Bahrain—possibilities for representation in expatriate communities. City & Society, 20(1), 79-104.

Parreñas, R. S. (2005). Children of global migration: Transnational families and gendered woes. Stanford University Press. Stanford California

Philippines – Department of Foreign Affairs https://dfa.gov.ph/distribution-of-filipinos-overseas Retrieved 7/29/2020

Philippines - Overseas Employment Administration. http://www.poea.gov.ph/programs/ programs &services.html Retrieved 7/14/2020

Rapport, N., & Dawson, A. (Eds.). (1998). *Migrants of identity: Perceptions of 'home' in a world of movement.* Bloomsbury USA Academic.

Seemann, B., & Fischer, M. (2015). *Migration and Refugees* (pp. 54-71, Rep.) (Wahlers G., Ed.). Konrad Adenauer Stiftung. Retrieved July 10, 2020, from www.jstor.org/stable/resrep10111.7.

www.ingramcontent.com/pod-product-compliance
Lightning Source LLC
Chambersburg PA
CBHW070349270326
41926CB00017B/4062